Workers' Rights

Trade Union Industrial Studies

This series makes two new types of provision in the area of industrial relations: first it is specifically directed to the needs of active trade unionists who want to equip themselves to be more effective, and second, the books are linked together in a series related to the requirements of existing training and education courses.

The books have been designed by a Curriculum Development Group drawn from the Society of Industrial Tutors; Michael Barratt Brown, Ed Coker, Jim Fyrth, Bob Houlton and Geoffrey Stuttard, together with Charles Clark and Francis Bennett of the Hutchinson Publishing Group. The Curriculum Development Group has prepared the guide lines for the texts and edited them so that they form a complete set of teaching material for tutors and students primarily for use on trade union courses.

The texts are issued in sets of four, together with an accompanying resource book which provides additional background material for tutors and students.

Trade Union Industrial Studies

This series is published in three sets, each consisting of four student texts and an accompanying resource book. This book includes additional teaching material for tutors and students, a recommended list of books and a further exploration of the subjects by the authors of the text.

Paul O'Higgins

Workers' Rights

Arrow Books

in association with the Society
of Industrial Tutors

Arrow Books Limited
3 Fitzroy Square, London W1

An imprint of the Hutchinson Publishing Group

London Melbourne Sydney Auckland
Wellington Johannesburg and agencies
throughout the world

First published 1976
© Paul O'Higgins 1976

Set in Monotype Times
Printed in Great Britain by litho by
The Anchor Press Ltd,
of Tiptree, Essex

ISBN 0 09 911890 4

Contents

6 Contents

Acknowledgements

I am deeply grateful for the help and advice I have received from Penny Butler, Bob Hepple and Dorothy Tanfield.

General Note

The law described here is the law of England and Wales. The position is the same, practically, in Scotland, although Scottish law has its own distinct system, with its own courts and legal terminology. Northern Ireland has its own labour law, and the legislation described here mostly does not apply there. It is likely, of course, that after a few years there will be legislation for Northern Ireland following the pattern of the Employment Protection Act and other statutes.

While this book was being written Parliament was in process of enacting the Employment Protection Act, the Sex Discrimination Act, the Industry Act and the Trade Union and Labour Relations (Amendment) Act. At the time of writing these Acts had not yet been finally approved by Parliament. When these statutes are law, dates will be laid down for when the new legislation is to come into force. This is particularly relevant in the case of the Employment Protection Act. The book has been written as though this legislation were fully operative; however, it is unlikely that all the provisions of the Employment Protection Act will be in force until some time after Parliament has given its final approval.

The Employment Protection Act is the most complicated labour relations legislation in this country, if not anywhere, so it is not possible here to list all the qualifications, limitations and exceptions to its provisions.

Preface

This book is about some of the problems facing a worker in his relations with his boss. What must the employer do for the worker? What must the worker do for his employer? What happens if the worker is dismissed? What demands can the worker make on the employer and upon the state? What protection has the worker against injury at work? What claims for compensation can he bring against the employer or against anyone else if he is injured?

This book is about the rules which govern the worker's relationship with his boss. It is therefore also concerned with other means, such as trade union action, which force an employer to behave in better ways towards his workers.

Because this book does discuss the law, readers may find the section (on p. 11) defining some of the legal terms used helpful. It might be a good idea to read that part of the book first.

This is not a legal book. It is a book about the treatment a worker may expect and demand from his boss and other people when he is in the work-place and when he is exposed to the risk of injury at work. It also tells him what he may expect and demand from his boss and other people if he is dismissed for any reason, including redundancy, or suffers an injury or contracts a disease at work.

By 'workers' rights' I want to describe two things. First of all I am going to talk about the demands which a worker may make if he asks the help of a court or a tribunal to see that he gets what he is entitled to. Secondly, I mean to describe those demands a worker may make upon his employer which trade union bargaining and trade union strength give him a reasonable chance of getting. These rights, even those which the law protects, are often the result of trade union action and can only be maintained by trade union action.

The relations between the individual worker and employer, and between unions and management, are power relationships. They involve a balance of power. As Professor Kahn-Freund has said in *Labour and the Law*, 'Law is a technique for the regulation of social power' (see p. 92). Law regulates the balance of power between the worker and his employer, between unions and management. It may tip the balance one way or another. It may help or hinder the growth and exercise of union power. At any one moment in time the extent to which the law helps or hinders trade unionism is itself largely a reflection of the balance of power in British society as a whole.

List of Main Statutes Affecting Workers' Rights

*Contracts of Employment Act, 1972: deals with notice and the written statement to be given by employers (pp. 15, 24, 35–6, 41–2, 56, 60, 75).

Employment Protection Act, 1975: deals with basic worker's rights, such as notice, maternity leave, etc. (pp. 36, 39–40, 41–2, 48, 59–60, 62, 68, 71–2).

Factories Act, 1961: deals with safety in factories, on building and construction sites, etc. (pp. 16, 82, 83).

*Health and Safety at Work Act, 1974: deals with general rules governing safety at work (pp. 16, 80, 82, 85–7).

Mines and Quarries Act, 1954: deals with safety in the mines (pp. 80, 82, 84).

Race Relations Act, 1968: (p. 58).

*Redundancy Payments Act, 1965: deals with redundancy compensation (pp. 56, 73).

Sex Discrimination Act, 1975; (p. 59).

*Trade Union and Labour Relations Act, 1974 (amended 1975): deals with trade unions, industrial action, unfair dismissal, etc. (pp. 19–20, 32, 33–4, 56, 62, 64–5, 69).

Truck Acts, 1831 and 1896: deal with payment of wages and discipline at work (pp. 49–50, 52, 54–5).

The Acts marked with an asterisk were amended by the Employment Protection Act, 1975.

Legal Terms

Worker

I have used this term throughout because it is the one used in practice. However, it is important to note that the technical term to describe the person who is entitled to the rights described in this book is *employee*. An employee in legal terms describes a person who has a contract of employment with an employer, but curiously there is no very precise definition of a contract of employment. Perhaps the most helpful thing to say is that those who are in business in their own right are not employees. Oddly enough, those who work on the lump are very often regarded by lawyers as being in business in their own right. The rights we have described have therefore (in most cases) no application to people on the lump.

Barrister

One of a small group of professional lawyers (about 3000 in Britain) who have the exclusive right to appear in the more important courts, that is, the High Court, the Court of Appeal, and the House of Lords, which are the 'Superior Courts'. They also give 'opinions' or advice on legal matters to solicitors acting on behalf of members of the public. They are the more specialized branch of the legal profession. A member of the public does not ordinarily have direct access to a barrister; he must usually first employ a solicitor who then gets advice from a barrister or engages him to appear in court.

Solicitor

The general practitioner of the legal profession. He gives general legal advice, writes letters, and appears in the lower courts, that is the County and magistrates' courts. Solicitors tend to be closer in touch with real problems than barristers.

Contract

A contract is an agreement which the law will enforce. In other words, if someone breaks the agreement the courts can award damages to the person who has suffered because of the breach and even on occasion order the person who has broken the agreement to perform it. Not every agreement is a contract, but most agreements where each side has bought the promise or act of another by a promise or act of their own is a contract. The essential element is bargain. Very many ordinary transactions are contracts. For example, if one buys a ticket on the bus, one is buying the promise of the bus company to be transported for a certain distance.

Civil law

This describes all those rules which, if not complied with, can only lead to civil remedies, that is, damages and possibly court orders, such as an injunction.

Criminal law

Those rules which if not complied with may lead to proceedings in courts which have the power to fine and/or imprison.

Injunction

An order of a court telling someone to do or not to do something. Disobedience may result in a fine or imprisonment.

Common law

A term used in different senses. In this book it is used to describe those rules created and developed by the judges as opposed to rules established by Parliament.

Legal aid

See Appendix 1.

Unlawful

An act is unlawful if it involves non-compliance with a legal rule. An unlawful act may be *civilly* unlawful, which means that anyone who has been damaged or inconvenienced by it may seek in the courts a *civil* remedy. This means that he can ask for damages or compensation, or sometimes he can ask for an order requiring the person responsible for the unlawful act to stop doing it, or even to undo what has been done. An unlawful act may on the other hand be *criminally* unlawful. This means that *anyone*, not only the person who has been damaged or injured, can take proceedings seeking a *criminal* remedy. The principal criminal remedies are court orders imposing a fine or a term of imprisonment.

Criminal courts

These are the courts in which criminal remedies can be obtained. They are principally the magistrates' courts and the Crown courts.

Civil courts

These are the courts in which civil remedies can be obtained. They are principally the County Courts and the High Court.

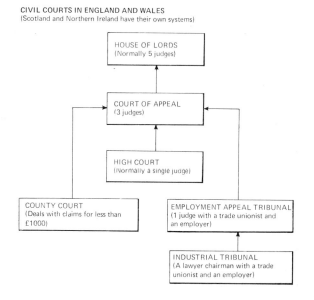

CIVIL COURTS IN ENGLAND AND WALES
(Scotland and Northern Ireland have their own systems)

HOUSE OF LORDS
(Normally 5 judges)

COURT OF APPEAL
(3 judges)

HIGH COURT
(Normally a single judge)

COUNTY COURT
(Deals with claims for less than £1000)

EMPLOYMENT APPEAL TRIBUNAL
(1 judge with a trade unionist and an employer)

INDUSTRIAL TRIBUNAL
(A lawyer chairman with a trade unionist and an employer)

1. 'Workers' Rights! What Bloody Rights?'

When I told Tom I was going to write a book called *Workers' Rights*, he said, 'Workers' rights! What bloody rights?' It was a good sceptical reaction and reflects some important features of British labour relations. British workers are used to relying upon trade union strength as the best means of obtaining the kind of standards they want in their lives. They expect nothing from the law or the lawyers as an act of charity. However, this attitude has its disadvantages. I remember one very famous trade union leader explaining to me how he protected the interests of his members when he argued their case for redundancy compensation in front of industrial tribunals. 'I speak loudly,' he said, 'I bang the table, and I get my way.' That man was not always helping his members; because of his ignorance of the rules which decide whether or not a worker gets redundancy compensation he lost many cases for his members which he should have won. It is very important, therefore, to be aware that legal rules may give workers certain benefits and advantages. It is important to know also that it may be possible to obtain these benefits and advantages by taking simple and cheap steps before a tribunal.

The many legal rules which give benefits and advantages to workers largely represent what previous generations of trade unionists have won by struggle, by industrial and political action. To regard them as irrelevant is to ignore the fruits of past struggles.

'What bloody rights?' Tom demanded. My answer is that the rules which govern the worker and his boss in the work-place do entitle the worker to expect a certain reasonable standard of treatment by his boss and by others. I want to describe the kind of things a worker is entitled to expect under the rules that apply in the work-place. These things I describe as 'workers' rights'.

2. The Rules of the Work-Place : 1

The rules which apply in the work-place are of many different kinds. We are unaware of most of them for most of the time.

Rules Made by Parliament

First of all there are rules made by Parliament. These we call statutes, or Acts of Parliament. They are the most important kind of rule because they override any rule made by anyone else that is not consistent with a rule made by Parliament. A good example is the Contracts of Employment Act, 1972, which tells the boss to give every worker a written piece of paper which *either* itself contains certain basic information about hours of work, rates of pay, etc., *or* tells him where he can find this information.

Delegated Rules

There are also rules which are not made by Parliament but by institutions or people who have been given legal authority by an Act of Parliament to do so. The local council issues bye-laws, which deal with many not very important matters such as dogs fouling the pavement. However, these rules may be important; they may, for example, limit the right to hold meetings in the town. Other bye-laws may regulate the conditions of young workers, such as news boys and girls. Parliament may give ministers the power to make rules. For instance, the Factories Act, 1961, gave the Secretary of State for Employment the power to make rules dealing with particular dangerous jobs. A large number of these rules, or regulations as they are called, have already been made and still remain law, although we have a new Act also, the Health and Safety at Work Act, 1974, governing safety at work. (As a temporary measure only, the old rules made under past statutes will continue to apply until they have been replaced by new, and I hope better, rules in accordance with the provisions of the Health and Safety at Work Act, 1974. See pp. 85–7.) Rules like these, made by various people, including ministers, and by nationalized corporations, local corporations and so on, are called delegated rules. Rules made by ministers as a result of power given to them by Parliament are called 'statutory instruments'.

Rules Made by Judges

These are rules made by judges of the most important courts, the House of Lords, the Court of Appeal and the High Court. It is a special feature of English law that judges can not only interpret rules made by others, but in the past could invent new legal rules themselves. Parliament did not give them this power. This is something the judges took for themselves at a time in the past when there were few parliaments. In the Early Middle Ages two people might come to a judge asking him to decide a dispute between them. Since Parliament had not laid down rules which might decide the problem (and nor had anyone else), the judge made his own rule to decide the question. In fact it was a sensible solution to a practical problem: where there was no law to decide a dispute the judge should be free to decide the dispute in whatever way he thought best.

However, the role of the judge is more complicated nowadays. Once one of the more important courts, which might involve several judges or only one, had decided a dispute in a particular way, later courts came to accept that they were bound to decide a similar dispute in the same way in the future. The way the earlier court had decided a case became law for other people in the future in similar situations. This rule-making and law-making power of the judges in England is an important aspect of the English system. One might expect that now that Parliament meets regularly and passes an enormous number of laws there would be no need for judges to be able to create new rules. The judges, however, do not always take this view, though some now do. Thus in 1964 the judges in the highest court in the United Kingdom, the House of Lords, created a new legal wrong (in a case known as *Rookes* v. *Barnard*), known as intimidation, in order to prevent a trade union taking industrial action of a kind which had been lawful in the past. Parliament had to step in to abolish intimidation for trade unionists engaged in industrial action.

Rules made by judges, sometimes called the common law, play a very important part in the relationship between workers and their bosses. For instance, judges laid down the rule that every employer must take reasonable steps to avoid exposing his workers to unnecessary risk of injury at work. It is the judges who have laid down that workers should obey orders given them by the management. And it is the judges who have made the rule that, if a worker makes a discovery or invention in the course of doing his job, the boss owns all of that invention or discovery and needs pay the worker not a single penny for his contribution. This is regardless of any effort or skill that the worker has contributed to the making of the invention or to working out an idea that improves productivity.

Rules Made by the Employer

These rules are made by the employer acting on his own initiative. He may say the work is to be done in a particular way. He can decide who does what job and when, though often only theoretically. He can forbid the playing of cards in the lunch hour. He can say that goggles should be worn when workers use a machine emitting sharp fragments of wood or stone.

Rules Made by a Worker and His Employer

There are rules made by agreement between an individual worker and his boss. These rules are known as the contract of employment. Of course, it is a fiction that the rules in the contract of employment are made by mutual agreement. In reality the individual worker must accept a job on the terms offered by the employer. The lawyers pretend that the terms laid down in this way by the employer are mutually agreed. However, the imbalance of bargaining power between the individual worker and his boss is compensated for by the bargaining strength of workers combined together in trade unions, and by the rules made by the workers amongst themselves. Sometimes, as well, the union may establish rules for the work-place.

Rules Made by Unions and Employers

In a sense the most important rules of all may be those rules which are in the form of a collective agreement mutually agreed between management on the one side and the union on the other, represented by a shop steward, a local official or a national official. These rules may cover many things, usually rates of pay, piece-rates, holidays, overtime rates, hours of work, safety, disciplinary rules, redundancy, dismissals, etc. They may also establish machinery for the settlement of disputes, such as a grievance procedure for individual workers, or the procedure to be followed when the union and management are in dispute.

These then are the principal kinds of rules which apply in the work-place. Notice that I have not said whether these rules are legal rules or not.

Rules Which Are Law

A legal rule is one which can be taken before a legal body, like a court or tribunal, which has to pay attention to it, such as by ordering somebody to pay compensation for not obeying it. However, some rules cannot be taken before a court or tribunal and nothing can be done by a court or tribunal about breaches of them.

This list gives rules which *are* legal:

1. Acts of Parliament.
2. Delegated rules made by people (or institutions) who have been given the power to do so by an Act of Parliament.
3. Rules made by judges.
4. Rules made by the individual worker in agreement with his boss in the contract of employment.

Rules Which Are Sometimes Law, Sometimes Not

The following rules are sometimes legal rules, sometimes not.

Rules made by the employer acting on his own initiative

Any rule which the employer makes under the authority given him by the contract of employment is a legal rule. On the other hand, if the boss suddenly puts up a notice to say that anyone who does anything likely to damage the reputation of the company may be dismissed, it is not a legal rule. Unfortunately, if nothing is done to object to a rule like this it may become a legal rule. The courts may say that everyone knew about it and therefore agreed to it. If the rule has been applied in the past on a few occasions, *and the workers involved did not object*, they may be taken as having agreed that it should be part of their contracts of employment.

Rules made amongst workers themselves

An agreement not to work more than so many hours overtime, and to pay the wages for overtime earned by working more than the agreed maximum number of hours into a common kitty, may or may not be a legal rule.

Rules made jointly by management and unions

It is often said that rules made jointly by management and unions in the form of a collective agreement are not legal rules, particularly if there was no clause specifying that such agreements were not legally binding. The problem has now been more or less resolved by the Trade Union and Labour Relations Act, 1974, which says that a collective agreement in writing is not to be a contract and is not to be a legal rule, unless the agreement itself states that it is to be a contract. This applies to collective agreements made before 1 December 1971 or after 16 September 1974. The position of agreements made between those dates not mentioned by the Trade Union and Labour Relations Act, 1974, is therefore uncertain. It is important to note that if a collective agreement establishes legal rules, they ordinarily apply only to management and the union, and not to individual workers. However, an individual worker's contract of employment can state that the rules of any collective agreement are to be part of it. If so, the rules of the collective agreement become legal rules for the individual worker and his employer (see also pp. 32ff.).

More detailed attention should be given to the special role of the judges and the relationship between the different kinds of rules. Also there is a difference of approach between someone practically engaged in labour relations and the approach of the lawyer, and the reasons for this difference may be very important.

The Judges

What is the role of the judges in labour relations? High Court judges in Britain have a special social origin. They are drawn exclusively from amongst practising members of the barristers' profession, a very small group of about 3000 people. Judges are upper and middle class, and most of them have been educated at public schools and at Oxford and Cambridge. Their lives while they were barristers were peculiar because barristers have little direct human contact with ordinary people. They may not even meet their clients before appearing for them in court proceedings. In other words, the class origins of judges and their lives as barristers prevent them from acquiring experience of the problems of the working class; they know very little about labour relations and do not understand much about the role of trade unions. There are notable exceptions from time to time, but judges are usually socially and politically conservative. This is not a matter of dishonesty or lack of integrity. Judges have a very wide freedom of action, including even a limited power to create new legal wrongs.

The big question is how would one expect them to act when deciding disputes between workers and management? This is the answer given by one of the most distinguished English judges of this century, Lord Justice Scrutton, in 1923:

The habits . . . the people with whom you mix, lead to your having a certain class of ideas of such a nature that . . . you do not give as sound and accurate judgments as you would wish. This is one of the great difficulties at present with Labour. Labour says 'Where are your impartial Judges? They all move in the same circle as the employers, and they are all educated and nursed in the same ideas as the employers. How can a labour man or a trade unionist get impartial justice?' It is very difficult sometimes to be sure that you have put yourself into a thoroughly impartial position between two disputants, one of your own class and one not of your class.

One of the consequences of this is that judges have tended to come down on the employer's side (as in *Rookes* v. *Barnard* in 1964). In practice the most important illustration of the damaging social role of the judges is that whenever Parliament enacts legislation to give some freedom to workers and trade unions so that they can take effective industrial action, the courts react by inventing new legal wrongs to prevent lawful strike action.

The Relationship Between Different Kinds of Rules

An Act of Parliament is the most important kind of rule and over-rides any other rule. Furthermore, however absurd or ridiculous the provisions of an Act of Parliament may be, they remain law and cannot legally be invalidated. On the other hand, many Acts of Parliament are dead letters because no one bothers to obey them and no one bothers to take the necessary steps to ask a court to enforce them. For example, the Shops Clubs Act, 1902, laid down quite sensible rules about occupational pension schemes. It says that it is a criminal offence for an employer to require a worker to join a compulsory occupational pension scheme unless certain conditions are fulfilled, such as minimum protection of the workers' rights in the pension fund, and also that 75 per cent of the workers must have said they were in favour of the scheme. An official inquiry in 1961 found that only a few thousand workers belonged to occupational pension schemes which complied with the law. The vast majority of workers belonging to compulsory occupational pension schemes in fact belonged to schemes which were unlawful.

Statutory instruments, or delegated rules made by ministers, are valid only if they are within the scope of their rule-making powers. For instance, if an Act of Parliament authorizes a minister to issue rules about safety in *factories*, any rule dealing with safety at work in any work-place *other* than a factory is not law. There are other grounds when a statutory instrument may be invalid. However, the principal ones are that the rule is concerned with a subject which is outside the range of subjects that the Act gave authority to make rules about; and that the minister did not follow some procedure laid down by the Act, for instance he failed to consult a group that he was supposed to.

Local authority bye-laws may be invalid on the same grounds, but they may also be invalid if it is not possible to know what they mean or are unreasonable (what is unreasonable is for a court to decide), or conflict with some rule of the common law.

Delegated rules which are inconsistent with an Act of Parliament are invalid.

Rules made by the judges (including the judges' interpretation of Acts of Parliament) are governed by special rules, because they depend upon what sort of court made them. No judge-made rule can override an Act of Parliament or a statutory instrument, although a court's interpretation of an Act of Parliament may defeat the purpose lying behind it.

A rule laid down by the House of Lords is binding upon the courts below it and upon the House of Lords itself (except in very exceptional circumstances).

A rule laid down by the Court of Appeal binds lower courts and binds the Court of Appeal itself, though not the House of Lords, which can overrule a rule laid down by the courts below it.

A rule laid down by the High Court binds the High Court and lower courts such as the County Courts and magistrates' courts.

But the Court of Appeal and House of Lords can invalidate any rule laid down by the High Court.

It is important to notice that industrial tribunals do not make rules which bind anyone. The Employment Appeal Tribunal makes rules which are binding on all industrial tribunals.

3. The Rules of the Work-Place: 2

Rules laid down by parties in industry, by employers unilaterally, or by agreements between workers and management in the form of collective bargaining, and any other rules established by workers and employers, unions and employers' associations, must legally give way to rules laid down by Parliament, by a minister, or by courts which have the power to make rules binding upon other people. However, County courts, magistrates' courts and industrial tribunals (and any other tribunals, such as National Insurance local appeal tribunals which decide appeals in applications for unemployment benefit) do not have the power to do anything except decide the particular cases in front of them. A decision made by an industrial tribunal is not a legal rule in the sense that it *must* decide another similar dispute in the same way. Of course if a tribunal decides a problem one way today it is likely that it will make a similar decision about subsequent cases of a similar type. *But the tribunal is not obliged to do so.* One can convince the tribunal that it would be better to decide the case before it today differently from the way it had decided a similar case yesterday. However, if one fails to convince the tribunal one *may* be able to succeed in an appeal.

Work-Place Rules in Practice

When a problem arises in the work-place about the rights or obligations of workers or management, there is a fundamental difference between what occurs in practice and the way a lawyer would look at the problem. If a dispute arises over overtime rates, or whether the employee is obliged to work overtime, a shop steward will look at past practice to see what in fact has occurred. He will look at the terms of the collective agreements (national, regional or plant bargains) applicable to the industry, and he will pay most attention to plant bargains; if these agreements are printed in a National Joint Industrial Council (NJIC) handbook he will examine that; if there is a company handbook, or employee handbook, he will look at that too. When he talks to management he will base his arguments upon these documents, upon past practice, upon common sense and upon what the interests of members demand. Management will do likewise, and a settlement may be arrived at after negotiation or after industrial action.

The Lawyer's View

A lawyer looks at the problem entirely differently. He will ask what are the *legal* rights and obligations of the worker and management. He will find his answer in what he calls the 'contract of employment'. What he means by the contract of employment is not what is ordinarily referred to in industry as the contract of employment. In industry every employer is required by the Contracts of Employment Act, 1972, to give to every worker a written statement which sets out some of the most important terms of the worker's employment. The employer either puts this information on a piece of paper or he may refer the worker to a collective agreement, a company handbook, a works rule book, or any other document where the required information can be found. Unless the lawyer is satisfied that collective bargains, the company handbook, past custom and practice, and so on, have become part of what he defines as the contract of employment, they have no bearing upon the *legal* rights and obligations of workers.

Does it matter that the lawyer's approach differs from that of the men who are engaged in labour relations? Yes, it may do, but it is usually only a problem when it concerns the rights of individual workers, for example, if a worker is claiming redundancy payment from his employer. Here, once it is established that the worker has been dismissed because of redundancy, he is entitled to receive compensation which is based upon the number of years he has worked with that particular employer multiplied by his weekly wage. But the question will arise, what is his weekly wage? Does it include the overtime pay he has received regularly for the past ten years? In commonsense terms it ought to, but when an industrial tribunal has to decide what the weekly wage is, it will ask what the weekly wage was *as laid down in the contract of employment*. Did the contract of employment require the employer *as a matter of legal obligation* to provide overtime, and did it also require the worker *as a matter of law* to work that overtime? If the answer is that although the worker was obliged to work overtime, the contract of employment did not make it a legal obligation for the employer to provide so many hours overtime each week, then overtime was not a mutual obligation of the contract. If there was no mutual obligation to provide and to work overtime, the amount of overtime pay earned regularly over the past years was not part of the weekly wage for the purposes of assessing the amount of redundancy compensation to be paid by the employer.

In other words, the difference of approach to workers' rights between a union official and a lawyer is really only relevant when a worker goes before a court or a tribunal. When a worker is seeking compensation for unfair dismissal or for redundancy, then it may be more to the point to start by asking what are the terms of the worker's contract of employment, than what happened in practice in the past to the worker (or group of workers) in this particular company.

Courts and tribunals give a great deal of importance in practice to the lawyer's concept of the contract of employment. It will be considered in more detail in Chapter 4.

4. The Contract of Employment

Definition

A contract is a *bargain* to which there are two parties or sides. In a bargain each side does something or promises to do something in exchange for an act or promise from the other side. If I promise to lend Mary £5 that is not a bargain, although there may be an agreement that I should lend her the money. It will become a contract if, in exchange for my promise to lend Mary £5, she agrees to do something for me, for example, if she agrees to lend me her pencil.

There is a contract of employment between a worker and his boss the moment the worker has agreed to work for the employer and the employer has agreed to pay wages for that labour. The agreement does not have to be in writing; it does not have to be formal. Usually a company advertises that it needs workers.

Mary sees the advertisement, or maybe a notice outside the factory gate, which says 'Hands wanted'. She sees the foreman (or someone in the personnel department) who may simply tell Mary what the wages are and that she is to start the following morning at 7 am. Once Mary and the foreman (or the person in personnel) have agreed that Mary is to start work for a certain wage, then there is a contract. Strictly speaking, it is not necessary for the precise wage to be mentioned. It is enough if there is an understanding or promise that Mary is to be paid.

Content

Now not a word may be said about holidays, occupational pensions, disciplinary rules, overtime, or even the basic hours of work. This is the surprising thing about the contract of employment. From the lawyer's point of view, once an agreement has been reached that Mary is going to work for wages, a contract exists containing terms describing the hours of work, holiday entitlement, etc., even though nothing may have been said about these things by either Mary or the foreman at the moment when they agreed that Mary was to start on the job.

How do we know what the terms of Mary's contract are, and how do we know what Mary's rights and duties are, when apparently nothing need be said about these things before a contract of employment is considered to come into existence? The problem is not difficult to solve if Mary is going to work in a unionized factory and if she is going to work in a job where there are already other women working. The answer in this case is that she is entitled to receive the same treatment as the women already doing the job; she has to work the same hours, and so on, as they do. In other words, if you start work in a job where there are already well-established terms and conditions, then your contract contains those terms and conditions.

The Terms

The terms of the contract may be either expressed or implied. For example, if the foreman tells Mary that her wages are to be £20 a week, there is then an express term in her contract that wages are £20. If nothing else is said, about hours of work, for example, then it is an implied term of Mary's contract of employment that her hours of work are those usual for a person doing the kind of work she is employed to do. Let us look in more detail at the express and implied terms in a contract of employment.

Express Terms

Express terms pose few problems. They will include not only the terms expressly stated by the foreman when he agrees with Mary that she is to start work the following day, but also any other terms he may refer to. The foreman may tell Mary, 'In our plant rates of overtime are fixed by agreement between management and the union.' If he says this it means that the overtime rates established by the collective agreement are also express terms in the contract. Sometimes the foreman may give Mary a company handbook and say that the basic rules of employment are to be found in the handbook. In this case the rules in the handbook are express terms of the contract of employment. But Mary must be given the handbook at the time that she agrees to work, or it must be made clear to her that there is a company handbook which she will receive later and which contains terms governing her employment. The foreman cannot give a worker a company handbook *after* he or she has begun work. Management cannot alter by its own act the mutual rights and obligations of either side under the contract; this can only be done by agreement between both sides.

SOMETHING TO DO WITH THE SMALL PRINT IN HIS CONTRACT

Implied Terms

Implied terms are more complicated. There are a number of different kinds of implied terms.

Terms implied by law

Over the centuries judges have said that every contract of employment is governed by, or has implied in it, certain rules. Every contract of employment must contain these rules. There are many of these rules, and they are imposed on the parties, on boss and worker alike, whatever their own private wishes or intentions may be. Examples include the following.

1. Every employer must take all the necessary steps to prevent his employees from being exposed to the risk of injury at work.
2. Every worker must obey lawful orders issued by his employer.
3. Any discovery or invention made by a worker while working for his boss belongs to the boss, and not to the worker.
4. The boss must pay the worker wages for his work.

If these contract terms are not complied with, sanctions for a breach of contract are available; these include a right to damages, as well as possibly the right to end the contract, or a court order making the person fulfil his obligation. In practice the first two are the usual remedies. A court will only rarely order someone to perform an obligation in a contract of employment, either express or implied.

Terms implied from the 'status' of the parties

This is new, and it can be illustrated from a modern legal decision. A lorry driver was involved in an accident for which he was responsible. The injured person sued the employer and recovered damages because of a rule that an employer is legally responsible for the loss caused to any third person by a careless act of his workers. In a case called *Lister* v. *Romford Ice and Cold Storage Company Ltd.* the House of Lords decided that the lorry driver must compensate the employer for the damages the employer had to pay to the injured third person, because there was a term implied in the lorry driver's contract of employment that he would reimburse his employer for any money the employer had to pay to a person injured by his carelessness. Where did the House of Lords find that term? One of the judges answered that they had found that term 'by considering the relation in which drivers of motor vehicles and their employers generally stand to each other'. In other words, the courts can decide that certain terms are to be implied into the contracts of employment of workers doing a particular job because the judges think these terms are essential to the relations between bosses and workers in that industry.

Terms established by applying the 'officious bystander' approach

Very often workers and employers do not bother to expressly state certain terms because they both understand perfectly well that they do in fact apply. For example, an employer advertises for lorry drivers. Michael applies for the job. Obviously both assume that they are agreeing that Michael can drive a lorry; that is, there is an implied term that Michael can do so.

How do we establish what these implied terms are? The court pretends to ask the question: 'What would this worker and this employer have replied if when the worker agreed to work for the employer, an officious bystander asked them, "Is there a term in your agreement that Michael must be able to drive lorries?" ' The court says that if the court would be justified in believing that both employer and worker would have replied with one voice, 'Yes of course we regard it as a part of our agreement that Michael is able to drive a lorry,' then a term to that effect is implied in the contract.

Terms which may be implied from custom and practice

Before any custom is regarded as part of the contract it must be 'reasonable, certain and notorious'. *Reasonable* means that it must be approved of by the judges. In one case the judge refused to allow a custom to be implied that involved paying non-unionists less than trade unionists, because he thought that the discrimination was unreasonable. The custom must be *certain*, which means that it must be able to be precisely defined. To say also that the custom or practice must be *notorious* means that it must be well known, for instance in Lancashire mills employers paid different rates for yards of cloth depending upon whether they were well or badly woven, and workers were held to be governed by this custom.

Not every practice can be considered to be part of the contract of employment. The court will ignore any practice which it decides is not reasonable, not certain, or not notorious. Many practices are followed by employers as management policy and not because they accept that they are obliged to behave in that way. Bonuses such as for productivity or for Christmas may be of this kind. If the employer makes it clear that he pays these bonuses as an act of generosity or charity, then it does not matter that he may have paid them for years, they never become part of the contract. The words used to describe the practice, like 'bonus', 'gift', 'gratuity', 'gratuitous', are not decisive, but they do suggest that the employer does not intend to follow it out of a sense of obligation, but is merely a matter of policy. Many years ago Tom Grieve of the Tobacco Workers' Union took an action against the Imperial Tobacco Company for withholding from him the usual Christmas bonus. The company withheld the bonus because Tom Grieve had taken part in a strike. The court decided that the mere fact that Imperial Tobacco had paid this bonus for many years did not make it a term of the contract.

Management policies often do not form part of the contract of employment. Thus if the company declares that it is its policy to promote 10 per cent of a particular grade each year, it is not likely to have become part of the contracts of employment of the workers in that grade, even if this policy has in fact been followed for many years. This will be for any number of reasons. First of all there may be no evidence of any agreement between the company and the employees; secondly, the agreement may not be in the form of the bargain; thirdly, describing the practice as a policy matter suggests that it is a practice that the management chooses voluntarily to follow rather than one followed by management because it accepts that it is contractually obliged to do so.

5. Collective Bargaining

Any trade unionist reading what I have said so far will be puzzled by one extraordinary omission. I have not referred to collective bargaining, and yet we all know that the most important method of establishing workers' rights and obligations is collective bargaining. Collective bargaining in Britain is curious because it is different from many other countries. In France, for example, the terms of the collective bargain often establish directly legal rights and obligations for workers. This is not so in Britain.

Definition

The obligations mutually established between the actual parties to the collective agreement by the union and management can become contractually binding, although this will be increasingly rare because of the Trade Union and Labour Relations Act, 1974 (see pp. 19–20).

A collective agreement does not directly confer rights upon individual workers and employers. This is because of a basic rule of British law that two parties (management and union) cannot by mutual agreement confer rights and impose obligations upon anyone else other than themselves.

The concept of agency forms an exception to this. If a group of workers agrees to give authority to a union or a shop steward to make a contract on their behalf, then the agreement so made is not an agreement between management and the union or shop steward but a series of agreements with identical terms between the management and each of the individual workers in the group who authorized the union or steward to act as their agent. This is rare, but is most likely to happen when a steward negotiates a settlement with management on behalf of a small group of workers. Mere membership of a trade union does not mean that a union official or shop steward can make agreements which bind the members in law.

The collective agreement usually indirectly establishes rights and duties for individual workers and employers by becoming a term in the individual contract of employment of those workers (look at pp. 26ff).

How Does a Collective Agreement Become Part of the Individual Worker's Contract?

By express incorporation

A term in the contract may state expressly that the contract incorporates the terms of relevant collective agreements. When the foreman agrees that Mary is to work in the factory he may hand her a copy of the company's agreements with the union. These agreements are then express terms of the contract of employment.

By implied incorporation

This takes two main forms. The court may take the view that it is so obvious that the employer and worker must have silently agreed or assumed that vital terms of the contract are to be found in the collective agreement that, if they had been asked about it at the time, they would have said something like, 'Of course we intend every matter we have not expressly mentioned to be governed by collective bargaining.'

On the other hand, it may have become a long-standing practice in the industry that terms are regulated by collective bargaining; the practice of following the terms of relevant collective bargains may have become custom. Another possibility is that the actual terms of a collective agreement may have stood for so long that the terms themselves of the collective agreement have become custom and practice.

Problems About Incorporation

There are a number of problems about incorporation.

Limitations

The possibility of express incorporation established by the Trade Union and Labour Relations Act, 1974, has been limited. Section 18 of this Act says that any term of a collective agreement which restricts the workers' freedom to take industrial action shall not become part of an individual worker's contract of employment unless the following conditions are fulfilled.

1. The collective agreement must be in writing.

2. The collective agreement must contain an express term stating that the term in the collective agreement about industrial action is to be incorporated into the contracts of individual workers.

3. The worker's own individual contract of employment must contain an express or implied term that the terms of the collective agreement are to form part of his individual contract.

4. A copy of the collective agreement must be available to the worker at his work-place for him to consult during working hours.

5. The trade union which is a party to the collective agreement must be independent; this means it must not be subject to the control or influence of the employer.

The translation problem

The second problem about incorporation is what may be called the *translation* problem. Not every term of a collective agreement that is incorporated into an individual worker's contract can impose legal duties or confer legal rights upon him. Many terms of collective agreements may not concern all workers. For instance, an agreement between management and ACTT that union members shall do something or be entitled to something from the employer, is not relevant to a worker who is not a member of ACTT even when the agreement becomes part of his contract. In other words, a term in a collective agreement about members of a particular trade union is not translatable into rights and obligations for someone who is not a member of that union. A provision in a collective agreement about what a union is to do or not to do cannot be translated into rights and obligations for individual workers.

Conflicting collective bargains

The third problem about incorporation is this: what happens if there are a number of different collective agreements, laying down different terms, all of which may be applicable to a worker? Strictly speaking the worker should get the benefit of all the relevant collective agreements. However, this is not what the courts have said. The courts have not allowed the worker to get the benefit of all relevant collective agreements. On the other hand, the courts have not explained how they decide which terms of which collective agreement are to be regarded as legally binding upon the worker because they have become part of his individual contract of employment. The position may be summarized briefly, crudely, but accurately, that so far the decisions suggest that the courts will only allow the worker to get the benefit of those terms in conflicting collective agreements which are least advantageous.

It is clear that it will not always be easy to be sure what the precise terms of the individual contract of employment are.

The Written Statement

I still have not referred to the document which is called in industry the contract of employment. A Bill was introduced in Parliament as early as 1823 because of the uncertainty about what a worker's rights and duties under the contract of employment are, which of course gives the employer greater freedom of action on his side to vary what he expects the worker to do. This Bill said that every employer was to give to every worker a written notice telling him what some of the more important terms of the contract were.

FOR MISS JONES HERE, THEY'LL SIGN ANYTHING

In 1963 that requirement became law. The relevant Acts of Parliament are now the Contracts of Employment Act, 1972, and the Employment Protection Act, 1975. These require that every employer shall give a written statement to a worker within thirteen weeks of starting work. The statement is to say:

1. The identity of the two parties, that is, the employer and the worker.

2. The date when employment began.

3. Whether employment with a previous employer counts as continuous employment with the present employer, and if so, on what date the previous employment began.

4. The date on which the information contained in the notice was correct.

5. Details about wage and piece-rates for the job.

6. A statement saying whether wages are weekly, daily, etc.

7. Hours of work.

8. Holidays and holiday pay.

9. Sick pay.

10. Occupational pension schemes.

11. Notice.

12. The title of the job; this is not the same as a job description.

13. Disciplinary rules which apply to the worker.

14. Reference to the grievance and disciplinary procedures, explaining how they work.

No information need be given about subjects nos. 4–10 if there is no term in the contract of employment about it. If the company has no occupational pension scheme and there are no terms in the individual worker's contract about it then no information has to be given about it. The employer may refer the worker to another document for the required information instead of giving him the information in the written statement itself.

It cannot be too often emphasized that this document is not in fact the contract of employment. It has no legal force at all. It is simply a piece of information about what the employer believes some of the terms of the contract of employment are. Although the document has no legal force, if there is no dispute between the worker and his employer about the accuracy of the terms it contains, it will be accepted by a court as good evidence of the terms of the contract of employment.

Traps

The written statement contains several traps for the worker. If when he receives the notice he signs a document to the effect that he agrees that the written statement correctly describes the terms of his contract, he will not be free in any legal proceedings to show that the employer got some of the details wrong. Secondly, if he merely signs a receipt saying that he has received a copy of the written statement, the receipt apparently makes the written statement into a contract (see a Court of Appeal case called *Mercer* v. *Gascol Conversions Ltd.* in 1974). This court decision was undoubtedly wrong. Courts are not very good at reading statutes and in this case the court misinterpreted the Act. This decision does mean, however, that workers must act on what the Court of Appeal says and refuse to sign a receipt for notices given them by employers, because in a dispute most courts will follow the Court of Appeal. The rule laid down by the Court of Appeal about workers signing receipts will be applied by other courts and above all by industrial tribunals. A union considering it important enough to fight the point up to the House of Lords might be able to persuade the House of Lords to correct the Court of Appeal.

Granted that the worker has not signed a statement agreeing that the notice he has been given under the Contracts of Employment Act is correct, and he has not signed a receipt either, if the document contains details which are inaccurate, he or his union should object at once. If he does not protest at once, then in a later dispute the lack of protest might be treated as evidence that he agreed with the accuracy of the document and he might then be prevented from showing that the employer had made a mistake.

Non-compliance

No penalty may be imposed upon an employer who fails to obey the law and give the required statement. There is therefore large-scale non-compliance with the law by small employers and employers in the non-unionized sectors. It is possible to ask an industrial tribunal to require an employer to give a written statement; if he refuses the tribunal can write one for him!

Who is the Boss?

One last word about the contract of employment. The parties to the supposed contract are the individual worker and his boss. Who is the boss? In most cases the employer is a company. The foreman is not the employer; the supervisor is not the employer; the personnel director is not the employer. All are employees of the same employer, the company. Of course the foreman, the supervisors, directors and so on are management; they represent the employer; they are agents of the employer, so that what they do or say will usually for legal purposes be regarded as acts of the employer. But in a legal dispute one does not sue the foreman or directors, one sues the company.

6. Basic Rights and Duties at Work: Statute

Workers' Rights

In a unionized industry, the rights and duties of workers reflect the balance of power with management and are the result of negotiation and industrial pressure and action. The law has a role to play here, since it sometimes provides machinery to encourage employers to comply with the results of collective bargaining. Three of the most important examples can be given here.

The Employment Protection Act, 1975, Schedule 11

This enables a union (or an empoyers' organization) to set in motion this machinery to bring into line an employer who is providing less favourable terms and conditions for his workers than those laid down by collective bargaining. The first step is to complain to the Advisory, Conciliation and Arbitration Service. If this does not have the desired effect, the complaint can then be referred to the Central Arbitration Committee of the Advisory, Conciliation and Arbitration Service which has power to order him to come into line with the collectively established standards. If he still fails to do so, any of his workers can sue him for breach of their contracts of employment, since an award of the Central Arbitration Committee of the Advisory, Conciliation and Arbitration Service by statute becomes a term in the contracts of employment of the workers concerned.

'Fair wages'

Secondly, every businessman who contracts to supply goods or services to a government department must accept certain terms which are laid down in the 'Fair Wages Resolution' passed by the House of Commons in 1946. They include a promise that the businessman, or government contractor as he is called, will give his workers terms and conditions which are at least as good as those established by collective bargaining. The contractor must also promise to recognize the freedom of his work people to join a trade union. These promises do not confer legal rights on these workers, but if they or their union complain the government department may persuade or pressurize the contractor to conform by threatening the loss of the right to do business with the government in future. The 'Fair Wages Resolution' is applied by local authorities when they place contracts with outside businessmen.

Statutory fair wages

Thirdly, in an industry which receives a state subsidy or financial assistance, or, like road haulage, requires a licence from the state, there is usually a statute legally obliging an employer to act as though he was a government contractor. This is called the system of statutory fair wages. If an employer in an industry to which this system applies fails to provide terms equal to those set down in collective bargaining, there is machinery to force him to do so. This machinery is broadly similar to that available in the case of Schedule 11 of the Employment Protection Act. An employer in road haulage may have his licence revoked or suspended.

Protective Legislation

Another kind of rule that is important in the work-place and may also reflect the balance of power in the community at large rather than within the enterprise between labour and management, is protective legislation. Protective legislation means here rules embodied in statutes (and also sometimes in statutory instruments) which establish minimum standards of employment. In Britain, unlike in some other countries, there are no statutes which lay down general minimum labour standards for all who work. There is no legally established minimum wage for all who work, although there is for wages councils industries (see p. 49). As a result, and also because of weak trade unions in certain industries, there are large pools of low-paid workers. Many of these receive less at work than they would be paid in social security benefits if they were out of work. There is no general statute forbidding employers from requiring workers to exceed certain maximum permitted hours.

In this country workers have traditionally relied upon collective bargaining to establish acceptable minimum labour standards. Historically, it is only where collective bargaining has not established them that there are statutory minimum labour standards. The hours of work of women and children are regulated by law in factories; this is partly because collective bargaining was at the time inadequate to do the job. Minimum safety standards were laid down by the Health and Safety at Work Act, 1974. This is because, for reasons which are far from clear, safety at work has not generally formed the subject matter of collective bargaining. In industries where wages are low and there is no effective trade union organization and no proper collective bargaining, there are statutory wages councils which have the power to make rules fixing legal minimum wages and holidays, as well as other terms and conditions of employment (Employment Protection Act, 1975).

Trade unionism in Britain has not always been as effective as it ought to be, and so the reliance upon collective bargaining has meant that the actual working conditions enjoyed by British workers have fallen behind the standards of other Common Market countries. Workers in Britain have less legal protection for public holidays and paid annual leave than in any other Common Market country, and many of their standards fall well below the minimum standards generally established by law (or by collective bargaining) elsewhere in the Common Market.

A Statutory Floor of Rights

There has been a change over the past decade. In 1963 the Contracts of Employment Act laid down minimum periods of notice for all workers. Since then there has been a trickle of legislation establishing minimum legal labour standards for everyone employed and not only those for whom collective bargaining has failed to do the job. British trade unions have so far been slow to use the statutory minimum standards as a basic floor of rights upon which to build and improve by collective bargaining.

Although the Contracts of Employment Act, 1963 (re-enacted and slightly improved in the Contracts of Employment Act, 1972) laid down minimum standards for notice, there were in 1975 still a number of collective agreements governing notice which merely repeated *without any improvement whatever* the provisions of the Contracts of Employment Act. In other words, the union bargained with the employer that he should do what he was already bound by law to do, instead of treating the legal minimum as the basis from which to bargain for better periods of notice. This is a futile form of collective bargaining. As statutory labour standards, for example about unfair dismissal, become more important, it is essential to use them as a floor upon which to establish better standards by collective bargaining.

The Employment Protection Act, 1975

The most recent statute laying down basic minimum standards for workers was the Employment Protection Act, 1975. This Act gave workers certain basic rights which can be enforced by complaining to an industrial tribunal. The standards and the rights established in this Act are often less than those enjoyed by workers who are effectively protected and represented by unions. Where trade unions are weak, ineffective or non-existent, the Act may help workers who work under bad conditions. Here are the principal standards laid down by the Act:

1. A right to guaranteed minimum payments by the employer in case of lay-off or short-time.

2. A right to be paid normal wages if one is suspended from work on medical grounds.

3. A right to maternity leave with a limited amount of maternity pay, a right not to be dismissed on grounds of pregnancy and the right to return to one's job at the end of this leave.

4. A right to time off, with pay, to perform union duties; without pay, to participate in certain union activities and to perform certain public duties.

5. A right, while under notice of dismissal for redundancy, to time off work to look for a new job or to make arrangements for training, coupled with an obligation on the employer to give advance warning of redundancy and to consult with the appropriate trade union.

6. A right to a written statement of reasons for dismissal.

7. A right to an itemized pay statement.

7. Basic Rights and Duties at Work: Contract

We must now turn to look at the contract of employment as a source of rights and obligations for the parties concerned.

History

The first thing to notice is that the contract of employment still bears the marks of its history. Until 1875 the rules of the contract of employment about the obligations of employer and worker were fundamentally unequal. Until 1867 any breach of the contract by the worker was a crime; between 1867 and 1875 only the more serious breaches were crimes. But at no stage was a mere breach of the contract by the employer a crime. During the period 1858–75 there were on average 10 000 prosecutions a year of workers for breaking their contracts, in England and Wales alone. Punishment could be imprisonment with hard labour for up to three months.

Not only was the law unequal but it was administered largely by magistrates, lay justices, from the employing classes, who often went beyond what the letter and spirit of a harsh law permitted and perverted the provisions of the law. To give a single example, in 1866 a potter was sent to prison for failing to go to work for his employer, although he produced a doctor's certificate stating that he was too ill to go to work. This biased law administered in a biased way was another factor which explains historically the traditional hostility of workers to law, lawyers and the courts (see also p. 21). In 1875 the Conspiracy and Protection of Property Act abolished the crime of breaking one's contract of employment, except for seamen.

Because a breach of contract by a worker was a crime, decisions of courts before 1875 about the employer's rights, especially his right to dismiss, should be irrelevant to modern conditions. But even since the Second World War decision of courts made before 1875 have been approved of by modern courts, although recently a few judges appear to have begun to realize that the old cases should be forgotten and ignored.

Inequality

The inequality of obligation in the old law has left a residue. Obligations are still not equal. The most important example is that it is not a breach of the contract of employment if management administers the affairs of a company so carelessly that it runs into financial difficulties, thereby causing redundancies. In other words, the employer is not subject to a legal duty to conduct the affairs of the company in a way which will not damage the economic interests of the workers. It is, however, the worker's duty in certain situations not to do anything which causes or is likely to cause economic loss to the employer.

The Judges' Approach

Some judges, who are socially conservative, tend to talk about 'masters' and 'servants', although Parliament ceased to use such words in statutes long ago. The vocabulary used by judges is significant for two reasons. It obscures the fact that most workers are employed by companies and not by individual employers; the modern employment relationship between a worker and BP or ICI is fundamentally different from the relationship in the nineteenth century of an agricultural labourer to the farmer who employed him. The judges ought to consider that because they are socially different, a different legal approach is justified. But all too often in employment cases judges tend to think of employers as human beings rather than as companies. It is not hard to realize that the motivation of a company may be very different from the motivation of ordinary human beings. Secondly, the master and servant approach, in so far as some judges still adopt it, is based upon old and irrelevant concepts of the duties of the worker, or 'servant' as the judge would call him. However, the judges are slowly changing their attitudes. In 1974 a judge in the Court of Appeal (Lord Justice Edmund Davies, in a case called *Wilson* v. *Racher*, said:

Many of the decisions customarily cited in these cases date from the last century and *may be* wholly out of accord with current social conditions. What would today be regarded as almost an attitude of Czar-serf, which is to be found in some of the older cases where a dismissed employee failed to recover damages, would, *I venture to think,* be decided differently today. (Italics added; note the caution.)

The Terms of the Contract

The following terms are generally to be found in any contract of employment. These are apart from the special terms for the particular employer and worker, which may be taken by express or implied incorporation (see p. 33), for example, from collective agreements, or which may be expressly agreed. These are the terms which the judges say are implied in every contract of employment.

The duty of cooperation

Both worker and employer must do nothing to prevent the performance of the other side's part of the bargain; there is a duty of cooperation. This does not mean that the employer must provide work. Ordinarily the employer's duty is to pay wages only. However, in certain circumstances the employer's duty extends beyond mere payment of wages. For example, where workers are paid on commission or work on a piece-rate, the employer must give the workers a reasonable opportunity to earn commission or wages. Occasionally it may be possible to imply that an employer is obliged to provide work, for example for very skilled people who need work to maintain and even develop their expertise.

The employee's duty of cooperation includes the duty to obey the lawful and reasonable orders of the employer. Certain forms of industrial action, such as the work-to-rule, and the go-slow, mean breaking this duty of cooperation. In the work-to-rule the problem is always what is the rule to which the workers are sticking, at least in the letter. If the rule is merely a term of the contract it must be interpreted in a reasonable way. Any interpretation which defeats the whole purpose of the employer's business may be regarded by the courts as not being a proper interpretation of the 'rule' at all. Therefore, since the worker is not complying with the terms of the contract, his action is a breach of the contract. On the other hand, some works rules which are invoked in working-to-rule are not themselves terms of the contract at all. They are simply orders given by the employer about how the work is to be done. In this case, since the employer can always change his orders, and the workers are no longer obeying his orders, they are breaking their duty to obey the changed orders. In other words, if the employer makes the 'works rules' on his own initiative, he can change them at will. On the other hand, 'works rules' which are bargained about collectively and which are then incorporated in the contracts of employment are terms of the contract and cannot be unilaterally altered by the employer. In this case sticking to the terms of the contract is all right provided the workers stick to whatever the courts regard as a proper interpretation of those rules. The duty of cooperation will usually prevent sticking to the letter of the rules, without regard either to past practice in the application of these rules or to their purpose, from being lawful.

The duty of care

Both worker and employer have a duty of care. The employer must take reasonable steps not to expose his workers to unnecessary risk of injury. For example, he must select carefully the equipment to be used by the worker. He must be reasonably careful to choose competent staff. And he must plan how the work should be done, including the layout of the work-place, to avoid obvious and avoidable risk of injury (for more details, see pp. 81–2). The worker on his side must exercise care and skill in doing his work, and try not to injure either his fellow workers or his employer's property.

The duty of fidelity

The employee has a duty of fidelity. He must be honest in the way he handles his employer's property. During working hours or outside working hours he must not do anything which prevents him doing the work he has contracted to do. This obligation goes very far; it is vague but extensive. Doing a part-time job in the evening for a firm which is in direct competition with one's daytime employer is a breach of contract. But it must be certain or strongly probable that the part-time job may damage one's employer's interests. The mere fact that the evening job is in the same kind of industry as one's daytime job is *probably* not sufficient. The worker's duty of fidelity means that he must not disclose confidential information to anyone outside the company, even after he has stopped working there.

Confidential information

It is not easy to say what confidential information consists of. It certainly consists of any information which might be economically damaging to the employer if it were disclosed, and it may go further. The courts have decided that the rule is broken if a trade unionist discloses to his union information about the profitability of the company that employs him, its wages and salary structure. This causes problems. The trade unionist can be protected by collective bargaining and, if the relevant terms of the bargain are embodied in the worker's contract, he is all right. However, if the information had already become public knowledge by being in the company chairman's annual report, which was reported in the newspapers, the information would no longer be confidential. (The rules about confidential information would make it difficult for unions to engage in effective collective bargaining if attention was paid to a case called *Bent's Brewery* v. *Hogan* which decided in 1948 that it was a legal wrong for a trade union to request its members to give it information about their employers' business activities, wage bill, turnover, etc. The right to such information can be given by a collective agreement between the employer and the union. Generally, the right to this sort of information and the restrictions on its use are now governed by laws, for example the Employment Protection Act and the Industry Act, 1975.)

Restrictions

Although the duty of fidelity makes it unlawful for a worker to use confidential information to compete in business with his former employer, employers increasingly put terms in the contract of employment which attempt to restrict the workers' freedom to work elsewhere in the same industry. These terms are said to be in restraint of trade; more accurately they restrict the worker's freedom to sell his labour where he wishes. These terms are lawful only if the employer can show they are necessary to protect some property interest, and if they impose upon the worker's freedom as little restriction as possible, in order to do so. For example, the list of names and addresses of the customers of a commercial enterprise has economic value. As a safeguard the enterprise can make it a condition of Mary's employment that for a few months she does not work for any other firm in the same town doing the same business. The wider the restriction geographically and the longer it is in time, the likelier it is that the courts will find it unlawful because it is greater than is strictly necessary to protect the employer's economic interest. This means that if Mary works in a job where she has no access to names and addresses the restriction will be invalid, because it is not necessary.

Remedies

Most of the duties imposed by the courts upon the parties to a contract of employment can be seen as applications of the principles of cooperation, care or fidelity. Breaches of these duties by one side entitle the other side to claim damages, and in serious cases the contract can be brought to an end. If a worker fails to fulfil one of his basic obligations this may entitle the employer to terminate the worker's contract, to dismiss him without notice (see pp. 56ff.). Employers do not usually sue workers for damages for breach of contract, but it has happened, and indeed was formerly quite common in the nationalized coal industry. (In Chapter 8 the other sanctions the employer may have when he thinks the worker is not fulfilling his obligations will be discussed.)

Wages

The basis of any contract of employment is that the employer must pay wages. Except in industries like agriculture, hotel and catering, which are covered by wages councils, there is no statutory regulation of the amount of wages; there is no legal minimum wage for industrial workers (as there is in France). There are a few statutes which affect wages, for instance, especially, the Truck Acts which have some important provisions (for truck legislation, see also pp. 52, 54–5).

How are wages paid?

The Truck Acts provide that workers engaged in manual labour, that is, *skilled as well as unskilled* workers whose job involves much use of their hands, must be paid in ordinary banknotes and coins. They can only be paid by cheque, by giro, or any other form of transfer, if they have *requested* their employer *in writing* to do so. Thus it is a criminal offence for an employer to insist that his workers shall be paid by credit transfer. Even if a worker has requested his employer in writing that his wages should be paid by credit transfer, he can withdraw the request and demand to be paid in current coin.

Deductions

Furthermore, the employer can make no deductions from the pay packet except those authorized by a statute (such as the

Truck Acts themselves), for example for food prepared and provided on the work premises, National Insurance contributions, PAYE. One important exception to this rule is that the employer can deduct from the worker's pay packet, if he requests, any sums of money which he owes or is willing to pay to someone other than the employer. In other words, the check-off is lawful, because it is a deduction of union subs for the benefit of some one else other than the employer. However, it is a criminal offence for the employer to make a charge for deducting union subs; if he keeps 5 per cent of the subs to cover his administrative costs it is a violation of truck legislation. The fact that a trade union may have agreed to this does not in any way alter the fact that the employer is breaking the law.

'Frustration'

It is sometimes difficult to be sure what the terms of the contract are concerning workers' rights to be paid some or all of their wages while they are off work because of sickness or accident. So it is important that this should always be regulated either by collective bargaining (which is then incorporated in the individual workers' contracts) or by express agreement. Sickness or absence from work due to injury which lasts for a long time, so long that recovery is unlikely in the near future, or in the case of a contract for an agreed period of time, so long as the employer is getting substantially less in the way of labour than he bargained for, automatically brings the contract to an end. The lawyers call this 'frustration'. Where a person is employed for a fixed term of two years and becomes ill shortly after starting work and remains unable to work for eighteen months, it is clear that the employer is not getting the substance of what he expected, namely the worker's work for two years. In this case the contract is clearly 'frustrated' and comes automatically to an end. It is not easy to know at what point in time prolonged sickness or injury 'frustrates', or brings the contract to an end.

A recent case, *Marshall* v. *Harland & Wolff Ltd.,* has indicated what factors may help to decide whether a contract has ended as a result of frustration. First of all, if there is a provision that the employer pays sick pay, then the contract is unlikely to come to an end by frustration until at least the end of the period for which it is payable. This will not apply where a worker is so seriously injured that it is clear immediately after the accident that he will never be able to return to work. Secondly, temporary absence from work due to sickness or injury is likelier to end the contract when the work itself is of a temporary character. Thirdly, if the job is responsible and the enterprise cannot carry on without a permanent replacement very soon, the likelier it is that even a short absence due to sickness or injury will end the contract. Lastly, if the worker has already worked for his employer for a long time his absence will probably have to be fairly prolonged before the contract automatically ends.

The most important practical point to bear in mind is that the union should bargain for sick pay to be paid by the employer for the longest possible period. This will help to prevent absence from work due to sickness or injury being used by the employer to argue that the contract has ended automatically. He will find this difficult if he is still paying the worker sick pay. Secondly, because there is no hard and fast rule about the length of absence from work or the degree of seriousness of injury or sickness which will 'frustrate' a contract of employment, the worker and his union should always challenge any dismissal for 'frustration' on grounds of sickness or injury.

8. Discipline at Work

The employer has a wide choice of sanctions available to him to punish a worker who does not behave satisfactorily. How far he may use them may be regulated by collective bargaining and by industrial pressure. Collective bargains about discipline which are part of the individual worker's contract of employment, give him the legal right to demand that the employer keeps to the contract. The worker also has open to him industrial pressure or action in cooperation with his fellow workers.

The most important and dramatic disciplinary sanction is dismissal (see Chapter 9). The employer may also sue the worker for damages for breach of contract, but this is rare. The most common disciplinary sanctions nowadays include fines, deductions, withholding of promotion or other benefits, and suspension. Because labour relations tend to be conducted without much attention to the legal rules, a good deal of disciplinary action is in practice unlawful and even criminal.

There are two main kinds of legal rules about disciplinary action at work. There are firstly the rules of the common, or judge-made, law. Secondly, there are statutes, for the most part the Truck Acts.

The Legal Rules

The legal position can be summarized as follows.

The contract

The employer may only lawfully impose sanctions which the contract of employment authorizes him to.

The contract of employment by implication and indirectly permits the employer to impose any sanction which does not involve taking away something which the worker's contract entitles him to. Thus, Tom Grieve (p. 31) was not entitled by his contract to a bonus, so it could be withheld by Imperial Tobacco as a disciplinary sanction.

A disciplinary sanction which means that the worker gets less than his contract entitles him to, is only lawful if the contract says so. This means that an unauthorized sanction would entitle the worker to claim damages from the employer for breach of contract.

Suspension

Suspension *with pay* is normally permissible because what it takes away, that is work, is not something which the contract entitles the worker to. All the contract entitles the worker to receive is wages. As long as he receives wages he has no further right to work.

Fines

Fines are an exception. The judges will say that any term which permits the employer to fine or make a deduction from the worker's pay packet for disciplinary reasons is invalid unless the amount of the penalty fine or deduction fixed by the terms of the contract can be regarded as a genuine guess at the value of what the employer has lost because of the worker's misconduct. For instance, employers may deduct half an hour's wages for being up to five minutes late. It is uncertain whether this is lawful, because it is hard to see that half an hour's wages is an honest guess at the value of what the employer has lost through the worker arriving late. If the worker is one minute late he loses half an hour's pay and if he is five minutes late he loses the same amount; but what the employer has notionally lost must be five times as great in the second instance. If so, the loss of half an hour's pay for being both one and five minutes late cannot both be honest guesses at the value of what the employer has lost. No union has ever challenged this in court, which reflects the fact that these matters may be better settled by negotiation. One should add that in negotiation a knowledge of workers' legal rights may be helpful to the union. Any fine or deduction which is so large, or is so out of proportion to the seriousness of the misconduct, that it has to be seen as a deterrent to misconduct (as opposed to compensating the employer for the value of what he has lost) is unlawful. The effect, however, is only that it is a breach of contract to impose such a sanction.

'Truck'

For workers engaged in manual labour (see p. 49) and shop assistants, the rules of the Truck Act, 1896, govern fines and deductions by employers for disciplinary reasons. It is a criminal offence for an employer to make fines or deductions for disciplinary reasons, including damage to materials supplied by the employer or other property belonging to him, unless all the following conditions are fulfilled:

1. There is a contract permitting these fines or deductions.
2. The contract is either in writing signed by the worker, or the terms of that contract are displayed in the work-place so that they can easily be read by the worker.
3. The contract must specify the acts for which fines or deductions may be imposed. Only acts or omissions which cause damage, loss, interruption or hindrance to the employer may be specified.
4. The amount of the fine (or deduction for damage to materials or property) must not exceed the employer's actual or estimated loss. In other cases the amount must be reasonable in the circumstances.
5. The fine or deduction must be in accordance with the terms of the worker's contract of employment.
6. The worker must be given a written statement about the amount of the fine or deduction and the reason for it.

7. The employer must keep a book in which he records the details of the fines and deductions.

The courts have permitted evasions of fines or deductions for damage to goods made by a worker. In a case called *Sagar* v. *Ridehalgh* (1931) it was held that a contract fixing different piece-rates for well-made goods and badly made or damaged goods was lawful. The explanation given by the Court of Appeal in this case was that truck legislation is concerned with protecting the wages earned by the worker. If a worker is paid 10p a yard for well-made cloth and $7\frac{1}{2}$p a yard for badly made cloth, and he makes two yards, one well made, one not, the wages due to him are $17\frac{1}{2}$p and there is no taking away from him what he has earned. For the same reason suspension *without pay*, if it is allowed by the contract, is not a violation of the Truck Acts.

9. Dismissal by the Employer

The Position in Practice

The ability of the employer to dismiss may ultimately depend upon the balance of power between unions and management. The precise rules about dismissal, whether it is for misconduct or for redundancy, and the procedure to be followed are often regulated in detail by collective bargaining. Sometimes the decision to dismiss may require the approval of a joint committee or of a works committee, although since unions regard their primary role as defending their members it is not common in Britain for unions to agree to a joint decision-making process whereby the union shares the responsibility for dismissal with management. But it does occur in some British firms. It is common to find jointly agreed rules about the procedure for dismissal, jointly agreed machinery establishing a right of appeal against dismissal, and customary practices such as 'first in last out', particularly in cases of redundancy. In practice it may not matter whether these have or have not become part of the individual worker's contracts of employment. However, if a worker has to go to a court or a tribunal to obtain a remedy arising out of a dismissal, it may be relevant to decide how far collective bargaining over dismissal and custom and practice has become part of the contract.

Legal Rules

Although the real position is in practice altered out of all recognition by collective bargaining, in theory at common law the employer enjoys a very wide power of dismissal. The common law power of the employer to dismiss has been modified not only by collective bargaining but also by legislation. In particular, the Contracts of Employment Act, 1963 (now 1972) altered the judge-made rules regarding notice; the Industrial Relations Act, 1971 (now partially re-enacted in the Trade Union and Labour Relations Act, 1974) introduced into British law the concept of 'unfair dismissal', and the Redundancy Payments Act, 1965, guaranteed a right to minimal compensation in cases of dismissal for redundancy. In this chapter two aspects of the law relating to dismissal, the common law concept of wrongful dismissal and the statutory concept of unfair dismissal, will be discussed.

Dismissal at Common Law

The common law rules about dismissal are as follows:

1. Provided the employer gives proper notice he may dismiss an employee for any or no reason.
2. Where there is serious misconduct (see p. 61) the employer need give no notice at all and can dismiss a worker on the spot.
3. If there has been no serious misconduct justifying summary dismissal, the notice to be given before the dismissal is lawful is either the notice stated expressly in the contract or the notice which is customary in the particular occupation. For example, it is customary for musicians to be entitled to one month's notice. Otherwise the notice must consist of a reasonable period. What constitutes reasonable notice depends upon all the circumstances of the case, including length of employment, the rate of pay, the responsibility and/or skill of the job, the difficulty a dismissed worker will have in obtaining another job, and so on. Reasonable notice will often run into many months.

4. If a contract is for a fixed term, there is no notice which can end the term prematurely, except in cases of serious misconduct.

5. The employer can end the contract by giving the worker wages in lieu of notice, which the worker has no option but to accept. This will be instead of giving the appropriate period of notice to end the contract.

6. There used to be no requirement that the notice specified in the contract had to be mutual. In many occupations the employer could dismiss at will, whereas the worker had to give three months' notice under the terms of the contract. Even nowadays the worker sometimes has to give a longer period of notice to end the contract than the employer need when he chooses to dismiss the worker.

Any dismissal of a worker which does not conform to these rules is known as 'wrongful dismissal' and entitles a worker to receive damages which roughly correspond to the wages he might have earned had the proper period of notice been given. The worker's right to receive damages for 'wrongful dismissal' are conditional upon the worker 'mitigating his loss'. That means that a worker dismissed without proper notice must actively seek to find another job. If he does find another job during the period which corresponds to the period of notice his employer ought to have given him, the amount of wages he receives during this period are deducted from the amount of damages the employer who dismissed him will be ordered to pay. If the dismissed worker does not look for another job the amount of damages he receives will be reduced by whatever amount the court thinks he might have earned if he had actively looked for a new job.

Statutory Protection

These common law rules have been modified by statute in a number of important ways.

The Race Relations Act, 1968

This makes it unlawful to dismiss a worker because of his colour, race, ethnic or national origins.

The Sex Discrimination Act, 1975

This makes it unlawful to dismiss a worker because of his or her sex.

The Employment Protection Act, 1975

This lays down minimum periods of notice to be given by the employer (except in case of misconduct sufficiently serious to justify summary dismissal). They are: one week's notice after four weeks' employment; two weeks' notice after two years' employment; and an additional week's notice for every additional year's employment after that working up to a maximum of twelve weeks' notice after twelve years' employment. The Act also gives any worker who has been employed for twenty-six weeks at the date of dismissal the right, upon request, to a written statement of the reason for the dismissal.

After the first four weeks of employment an employee must give the employer not less than one week's notice, unless the employer has been guilty of a serious breach of the contract of employment, for instance, has refused to pay wages due.

It is important to note that the periods listed above are the minimum periods. The Act does not say what the periods ought in fact to be. This is left to custom, to mutual agreement (including incorporation of terms about notice established by collective bargaining), or it remains a reasonable period.

In practice some workers get less notice than they are entitled to legally because of the widespread belief that the Act says what the periods of notice are to be. Furthermore, the actual periods of notice expressly agreed in the contract or by collective bargaining very often correspond only to the minimum periods laid down in the Act. Had the notice not been specified, many workers would have been entitled to longer periods by applying the principle of 'a reasonable period of notice'. In other words, in the past it was common for no period to be expressed, and then the worker was entitled to a reasonable time. The Act has encouraged employers to be more specific, and in some cases this has meant less time than the worker had previously been entitled to.

Wages in Lieu

The Contracts of Employment Act, 1963 (re-enacted in 1972), introduced two novelties about the worker's rights in case of dismissal. Under the common law the worker had no option but to accept wages given in lieu of notice; now under the Act the worker must agree to forgo his statutory rights to notice. He now can *agree to accept* wages in lieu of notice, but he can insist upon the contract not coming to an end until the proper period of notice has run out. This means the worker may either serve out his notice, or, if the employer does not want the worker on his premises, then the worker can insist upon being paid weekly until the period of notice runs out. This possibility confers certain benefits upon the worker, for example for National Insurance purposes.

The 1972 Contracts of Employment Act guarantees the worker a minimum income for the period of notice, at least where the period set down in his contract is not significantly longer than the minimum set down by the Employment Protection Act. Under common law, if a worker was ill during the period of notice, or absent from work as a result of an accident, the contract might have provided that the worker should receive nothing or only a small sum by way of so-called sick pay. The 1972 Act guarantees that the employer must pay the worker during notice (even if he is absent because of holidays, sickness or injury), and he has a right to receive the statutory minimum wage. The exact wage depends upon a number of factors (listed in Schedule 1 of the Act). The simplest example is a worker *who works regular hours* and is paid at a flat rate, who is entitled to be paid his normal wage for the statutory period of notice. If he also gets sickness or injury benefit from the National Insurance scheme, the employer must still pay him his full normal wage, unless he has a special sick-pay rate calculated with reference to sickness or injury benefit. In this case he only has to make up the difference between the amount of sickness or injury benefit payable and the amount of the normal weekly wage.

Remedies

As indicated already, if a worker is dismissed in breach of the rules (on p. 62–3) on wrongful dismissal, he can recover damages from the employer. In exceptional cases the worker is able to obtain an order from the courts that his job still belongs to him, and can thus prevent the employer from treating him as dismissed. This applies in jobs governed by statute, for instance registered dock workers, and may possibly apply in public employment. Actually, the precise categories of job which would entitle the worker to get his job back are unclear.

One of the least satisfactory features of the common law on dismissal is that it is quite impossible to say in advance of legal proceedings exactly what kind of misconduct will justify dismissal without notice. All one can say is that the more serious the inherent nature of the misconduct the likelier it is that summary dismissal is justified. It is not the consequences of the misconduct that matter. Past cases are of little help because they tend to reflect the subjective socially conditioned views of what judges in the past have regarded as serious misconduct by 'servants'.

In the latter half of the twentieth century and in an industrial context a different approach may be required and even applied by the courts. There are no clear rules that can be laid down now. Misconduct outside the work-place and working hours may still justify summary dismissal, although this will not often be so. Dishonesty is likely to justify summary dismissal even if it is not so serious as to constitute a crime. Bad language and talking back to the boss used to be strongly disapproved of by judges. However, modern judges will probably adopt a more rational attitude. A view is even emerging, expressed by Lord Justice Edmund Davies, that worker and employer owe each other mutual respect, that is, the courts do not necessarily regard the employer as having unlimited authority. Thus not every act of disobedience by a worker will nowadays justify summary dismissal.

The employer may insert the works rules, which he has unilaterally drawn up, as terms in the contract of employment. If those works rules expressly provide that certain otherwise fairly trivial acts shall be dismissable offences, then they are dismissable and will justify a summary dismissal, although it will not necessarily be a fair dismissal (see p. 57). In other words, the employer can add to his inherent power to dismiss for serious misconduct by inserting a term in the contract of employment which gives him a more unlimited power of summary dismissal.

10. Unfair Dismissal

The most important development in restricting the employers'
freedom to dismiss workers has been the concept of 'unfair dismissal', now found in the Trade Union and Labour Relations
Act, 1974, and the Employment Protection Act, 1975. The basic
principle is clear enough. No employer should be entitled to dismiss a worker for any reason that will not stand up to examination
by some public authority. Of course, the details are more complicated than that.

Basic Rules

The basic rules about unfair dismissal run like this. A dismissal is
unfair unless the employer can show that the reason for dismissing
the worker falls under one of the following heads.

    1. Misconduct.
    2. The worker's lack of capability or qualifications to do the
job he is employed to do.
    3. Retaining the worker in the job would mean that either the
worker or the employer would be breaking a statutory restriction.
A good example is the fact that the 1974 Act permits a union by
agreement to restrict the employer's right to employ a non-
unionist. A non-unionist can be dismissed because retaining him

in employment would involve the employer in breaking an obligation under the Act.

4. Other substantial reasons. This is a real catch-all; it enables personal considerations to justify dismissal, for instance, psychological incompatibility between a worker and individual members of management.

5. Redundancy.

6. National security.

7. Striking. Only if the dismissed striker can show he was victimized, not treated in the same way as other strikers, is it possible for him to claim for unfair dismissal. Britain is one of a declining number of countries in which the legal right to strike is denied, and the employer has the right to penalize a worker for having struck, regardless of the merits of the strike action.

In all these cases (except no. 6) the employer must also show that his reasons were genuinely sufficient to justify dismissal.

The Code of Practice (paras. 130-33)

The National Industrial Relations Court, under the Industrial Relations Act, established certain basic principles about whether the employer has acted reasonably which continue to be applied. The circumstances to be considered will include the Code of Practice issued in connection with the Industrial Relations Act. The Code contains a number of provisions about dismissals, in the form of advice to employers. Concerning dismissals for redundancy, the Code advises that employers should give as much warning as possible to workers of impending redundancies; help should be given in obtaining new jobs; there should be consultation with unions to seek to avoid unnecessary redundancy and to cushion its effects. As for dismissals for other reasons, the employer is responsible for making sure that workers are aware of the company's disciplinary rules, in particular what kinds of conduct may give rise to dismissal. The Code contains the Government's advice about the procedure to be followed for disciplinary and dismissal proceedings (see paras. 130–33).

The provisions of the Code

Management should ensure that fair and effective arrangements exist for dealing with disciplinary matters. These should be agreed with employee representatives or the trade unions concerned and should provide for full and speedy consideration by management of all the relevant facts. There should be a formal procedure except in very small establishments where there is close personal contact between the employer and his employees.

Management should make known to each employee its disciplinary rules and the agreed procedure, and the type of circumstances which can lead to suspension or dismissal.

The procedure should be in writing and should specify who has the authority to take various forms of disciplinary action, and ensure that supervisors do not have the power to dismiss without reference to more senior management. It should give the employee the opportunity to state his case as well as the right to be accompanied by his employee representative. It should provide for the right of appeal, wherever practicable, to a level of management not previously involved. It should also provide for independent arbitration if the parties to the procedure wish it.

In cases of misconduct, the disciplinary action to be taken will depend on the circumstances, including the nature of the misconduct. But normally the procedure should operate as follows.

The first step should be an oral warning or, in more serious cases, a written warning setting out the circumstances. No employee should be dismissed for a first breach of discipline except for gross misconduct. Action on any further misconduct, for example, final warning, suspension without pay or dismissal, should be recorded in writing. Details of any disciplinary action should be given in writing to the employee and, if he so wishes, to his employee representative. No disciplinary action should be taken against a shop steward until the circumstances of the case have been discussed with a full-time official of the union concerned.

Why is the Code relevant?

The answer is that the Trade Union and Labour Relations Act, 1974, says that a breach of the Code is not of itself an unlawful act, but that when an industrial tribunal considers any part of the Code relevant, it is bound to take it into account. This has been interpreted to mean that when a tribunal is deciding whether an employer has acted reasonably in beating a reason as sufficient to justify his terminating a contract, it will take into account whether the employer has followed the advice of the Code. This means that if a worker has been guilty of misconduct his dismissal is prima facie fair, but if in deciding to dismiss him the employer failed to follow the procedure (laid down in para. 133 of the Code), that fact *may* mean that the dismissal will be treated as unfair.

Consistency

Furthermore, the question whether a dismissal is fair or unfair will include considering whether the employer was acting consistently with his own past practice. If he has not in the past enforced the works rules, he cannot suddenly start enforcing them by dismissing people. Suppose the employer has always allowed time for his workers to make representations to him about proposed changes in the piece-rate or other working practices. Then on one occasion the employer simply announces a change without allowing time for representations, and dismisses a worker who refuses to accept it; then that dismissal is likely to be regarded as unfair. (This example depends in part upon whether the employer has authority under the contract of employment to alter working practices, including the piece-rate.)

   Whether the employer has acted in accordance with good industrial relations as understood by the industrial tribunal also has to be taken into account.

Acting Reasonably

One interesting case shows how far the concept of unfair dismissal has been developed by the tribunals and courts. In *Vokes Ltd.* v. *Bear* (1973) an employee of a company, which was itself part of the Tilling Group of 300 companies, was dismissed for redundancy (which by itself suggested the dismissal might be fair), but the employing company failed to show that it had acted reasonably in all the circumstances. First of all, no warning of impending redundancy had been given, no time off during working hours had been given to allow the employee to look for another job, and the company had made no effort to help him find another job. All these are requirements of the Code. Furthermore, the company had not done what 'in all fairness and reason they should do, namely, to make the obvious attempt to see if the employee could be placed somewhere else within this large group.' This was a surprising condition of fairness of dismissal. The Tilling Group had no centralized personnel department or other machinery for providing services for all the companies in the group. There was no easy way of finding out whether there was a suitable vacancy elsewhere in the group. The tribunal took the view that the total failure of the employing company to make any enquiries within the group of itself made the dismissal unfair. The implications of this decision may be far-reaching. It may mean that if a local authority dismisses someone for redundancy it must enquire amongst other local authorities to see if there is a suitable vacancy, otherwise the dismissal may not be fair. What is not clear is what relationship must exist between employers who belong to a group of employers for the obligation to make enquiries within the group to arise. So far the courts have sought to minimize the implications of *Vokes Ltd.* v. *Bear*.

Remedies

Once the fact that the dismissal is unfair has been established, what happens then? Cases of unfair dismissal are heard by industrial tribunals, which consist of a lawyer as chairman and two non-lawyers who have some experience of labour relations.

Reinstatement or re-engagement

These tribunals must first of all decide whether to make an order of reinstatement or re-engagement. Re-engagement means getting a job again with the former employer, not necessarily the same job, or, if the same job, not on the same terms, and usually involves the loss of certain seniority rights; reinstatement means getting the old job back on the same terms, including arrears of wages for the period between dismissal and return to the job, and with no, or only small, loss of seniority rights. An order will be made if reinstatement or re-engagement is practicable. But to order the re-engagement of a non-unionist dismissed because of union pressure is not practicable. If the order is made and complied with that ends the matter.

Compensation

If no order is made, or an order has not been complied with, the tribunal must consider the amount of the compensation that should be paid by the employer. The fact that a worker has been unfairly dismissed because of union pressure is irrelevant so far as the employer's liability to pay compensation is concerned. If the employer has refused to act on an order this is likely to increase the amount of compensation payable.

The amount of compensation payable to an unfairly dismissed worker is governed by the following rules. If the employer refuses to comply with an order for reinstatement or re-engagement and he cannot show that it is not reasonably practical to comply with it, then he may be ordered to pay 'punitive damages' to the worker. The maximum amount is 52 weeks' pay if the reason for the dismissal is the race, sex or trade union affiliation of the worker. For dismissals for any other reason, the maximum is 26 weeks' pay. The tribunal will generally make a provision in its order for reinstatement or re-engagement for wages lost by a dismissed worker between the date of dismissal and the date of going back to work. If the worker does not get his job back then he is entitled to a basic award and a compensatory award. These are in addition to any punitive damages he may have received. The basic award is a minimum of two weeks' pay or an amount equivalent to what he would have received had he been dismissed for redundancy instead of being unfairly dismissed (whichever is the greater). The maximum amount of basic award recoverable is £2400. It is payable whether or not the worker has suffered any financial loss due to the dismissal.

In addition, the dismissed worker, if he has suffered financial loss, is entitled to a compensatory award of up to a maximum of £5200. Compensation will normally be awarded under the following heads.

1. *Immediate loss of wages.* This will include as a basic minimum the amount the worker would have been paid had proper notice been given. If notice or wages in lieu of notice have been given then no more is given under that head. Loss of wages principally means an amount representing the wages lost between the date of dismissal and the date of obtaining another job (or the date of the hearing by the tribunal if the worker is still unemployed).

2. *Loss of prospective wages* where the worker is still unemployed or employed at a job paid at a lower wage than the job from which he was dismissed.

3. *Loss of certain statutory rights* which depend upon the length of service. If a worker is dismissed after ten years' work, then at that moment, if he has been dismissed for redundancy, he might have been entitled to claim £300–400 redundancy compensation. Since he has been unfairly dismissed, when he takes a new job with another employer he is not protected for the first two years of employment in respect of entitlement to redundancy compensation against dismissal for redundancy by the new employer. Accordingly the worker will get a small sum, as a rule of thumb half the amount he would have got had he been dismissed for redundancy (more if the tribunal thinks that if he had not been unfairly dismissed he might well have been dismissed for redundancy in the near future). Of course, if the worker is entitled to redundancy compensation and has received it, he will get nothing extra in respect of loss of protection against future redundancy. Again the statutory right to minimum periods of notice depends upon length of service; starting off with a new employer the minimum period to which the worker is entitled under the Employment Protection Act is very short, so that a smallish sum may be awarded for loss of that statutory protection.

4. *Occupational pension rights.* Except where pension rights are transferred or preserved under the Social Security Act, 1975, and this will be increasingly the case, a sum will be awarded for loss of the value of his prospective pension; the worker will also be entitled to receive back both his own contributions as well as his employer's.

5. *Hurt feelings*: although nothing will be given for them, if the manner or fact of the dismissal is such as to make it particularly difficult for the worker to obtain a new job this will be taken into account.

If the worker has by his own conduct contributed to the dismissal or its unfairness, then the tribunal may reduce the amount of compensation it will award him. The amount in any case awarded in respect of loss of wages will be net (that is, after allowing for deductions for National Insurance and PAYE); furthermore, unemployment benefit will also be deducted from the sum awarded if the dismissed worker has received or was entitled to claim unemployment benefit. A worker dismissed unfairly may also have the amount of compensation reduced if he has not actively searched for a new job. This may conflict with proper industrial relations practice. When a worker is dismissed unfairly and the union is actively negotiating with the employer to get his job back or is putting pressure on the employer to take him back, it weakens the union's tactical position if the dismissed worker has taken another job in the meantime.

Although the Trade Union and Labour Relations Act says that every worker 'has a right not to be unfairly dismissed', this is not strictly true. What the law does is to say that no employer can be legally forced to take back a worker he has dismissed unfairly; he must pay him compensation. In other words, the law fixes the price at which an employer has the right unfairly to dismiss a worker.

Invalid Reasons for Dismissal

There are a number of reasons which will always render a dismissal unfair.

One of these is what is called an 'inadmissible' reason. There are two of these. The first is that the worker is, or proposes to be, a member of an independent trade union, or participates in its activities, or refuses to join a trade union which is not independent. The second is if in a closed shop or union membership agreement he refuses to join an appropriate independent trade union on grounds of religious objection to joining any union, or on reasonable grounds refuses to join an appropriate trade union.

Another invalid reason for dismissal is a redundancy situation: the worker is dismissed for redundancy but has been selected for dismissal out of a number of workers and the reason for his selection is an inadmissible reason, or he is selected for dismissal in breach of a customary practice or an agreed procedure and there are no special reasons justifying departure from the custom or procedure.

'Wrongful' Dismissal and 'Unfair' Dismissal

Given that there are two different concepts, 'wrongful' dismissal and 'unfair' dismissal, what is the relation between them? Are both still relevant? Has not the concept of unfair dismissal totally replaced that of wrongful dismissal? Strangely enough, both remain relevant. Whenever for one reason or another a claim for unfair dismissal cannot be brought or where the compensation for unfair dismissal does not cover a worker's financial loss, a dismissed worker can still consider whether he can claim for wrongful dismissal.

Claiming for unfair dismissal

A worker *cannot* claim for unfair dismissal if:

1. He has not been continuously employed for twenty-six weeks by the employer who has dismissed him. During the first six months of employment the only possible claim that can usually be brought is a claim for wrongful dismissal.

2. He has failed to bring his claim within three months of dismissal. He cannot bring a claim for unfair dismissal after that date unless he can show it was not reasonably practicable for him to do so. The time limit for bringing a claim for wrongful dismissal is six years.

Certain people cannot, even if employed for six months, bring a claim for unfair dismissal. They are those who are employed for less than sixteen hours a week except where they have been employed for five years for not less than eight hours a week.

It will happen that even though a claim for unfair dismissal has been brought, the statutory limit of £11 760 (that is, a basic award of £2400 and a compensatory award of £5200), plus punitive damages of up to £4160 (see p. 77–8), upon the amount of compensation which can be recovered from an employer, will mean that unfair dismissal will not compensate for the full amount lost, if the employee's economic loss caused by the dismissals is much greater than £7600 and there is no award of punitive damages. In these cases, for instance someone employed in management, it may be possible to recover further damages in the form of a claim for wrongful dismissal.

Although claims for wrongful and unfair dismissal may arise out of the same facts, they are not alternatives. Each is governed by its own rules so that a dismissal may result in successful claims under both heads, or under only one. An unfair dismissal is not necessarily a wrongful dismissal or vice versa. If a worker has successfully brought a claim for unfair dismissal he will not get both amounts of compensation in full, even if he is successful in a claim for wrongful dismissal. The compensation he receives for unfair dismissal will contain an element representing loss of wages; in so far as a claim for wrongful dismissal is primarily a claim for lost wages, if he has recovered in the first case some or all of the wages lost, those will notionally be deducted from the damages ordered to be paid to him by the employer in the second case. The converse will apply equally, although it is important to remember that compensation for unfair dismissal includes loss other than lost wages.

Applications of the Rules

There are anomalies arising out of the existence of two claims for the same dismissal. Firstly, they are tried in different places: a claim for wrongful dismissal will be heard in the County Court (exceptionally in the High Court), whereas industrial tribunals hear claims for unfair dismissal. Secondly, legal aid is available to help a worker in bringing a claim for wrongful dismissal. There is no state legal aid for a worker bringing his claim before an industrial tribunal (except for the £25 Scheme, see pp. 92–3), although this is not very important practically to a union member, whose union will often provide him with legal assistance.

The appeal systems for the two claims are different. If a worker claims for unfair dismissal, there is a right of appeal, *on a question of law only*, to the Employment Appeal Tribunal. For wrongful dismissal there is a right of appeal from the County Court to the Court of Appeal and onwards to the House of Lords. Here the facts as well as questions of law can be argued about. In an unfair dismissal appeal the only question on appeal is whether the tribunal has got the law wrong. The fact that the Employment Appeal Tribunal might have taken a different view of the evidence is irrelevant unless the Appeal Tribunal is satisfied that the evidence was such that the industrial tribunal could not reasonably and honestly have come to the conclusion about the facts that it purported to do. The Employment Protection Act does authorize the Lord Chancellor to transfer to industrial tribunals the right to decide all claims arising out of breaches of contract of employment (other than claims arising out of personal injuries). Once claims arising out of both wrongful and unfair dismissal are decided in the same proceedings before an industrial tribunal, the difficulties facing workers who wish to bring legal claims will be slightly eased.

Weaknesses

It should be emphasized that there are many weak points in the present concept of unfair dismissal. Apart from the points already discussed, like the dismissal of strikers being fair, the level of compensation is too low. No compensation may be payable to an unfairly dismissed worker who has been given proper notice and has got a new job at reasonable rates of pay. Furthermore, it has been decided that the employer is not bound by the reason he gives at the time of dismissal. The Employment Protection Act for the first time makes it compulsory for an employer, if requested, to state the reasons for a dismissal. The Act does not, apparently, alter the rule that the employer is not bound by the reasons he gives at the time of dismissal. If the facts might have justified a fair dismissal and those facts were known to both sides at the time of dismissal, those facts may make the dismissal fair.

The excluded classes are too wide: a worker is not normally protected against unfair dismissal until he has worked for six months; he is not protected after normal retiring age; and he is not protected unless he normally works for sixteen hours a week for an employer, or eight hours a week for five years. This effectively excludes large numbers of part-time women workers from protection.

11. Dismissal and Redundancy

We have seen that a worker who has been dismissed may be able to claim compensation for being dismissed without proper notice. He may be able to claim for unfair dismissal. He may also claim a redundancy payment. The matter may of course be settled by a mutual agreement between union and management over the procedure for selecting people for redundancy and the amount of compensation payable. But if there is no negotiated settlement the worker should claim a redundancy payment *from his employer* in writing within six months of his dismissal. If the employer agrees to make a satisfactory payment then no further steps need be taken. The matter can be referred to an industrial tribunal if the worker would get less under the terms of the negotiated settlement than under the Redundancy Payments Act, 1965, or if the employer fails to make a satisfactory payment. If the worker has not already served a written notice upon his employer, the claim must be referred to the industrial tribunal within six months of his dismissal.

The following conditions must be fulfilled if a claim for re-dundancy payment before an industrial tribunal is to succeed.

Dismissal

The worker must show that he has been dismissed. For the pur-poses of a redundancy payment and of a claim for unfair dismissal, dismissal includes the following circumstances. The employer, with or without notice, terminates the contract. The employer does some act which is a serious enough breach of the contract of employment to justify the worker himself terminating the contract; this is sometimes called 'constructive dismissal'. In a fixed term contract, the period fixed for employment comes to an end without the contract being renewed. Certain other events constitute special cases of dismissal, for instance the death of an individual employer, or the dissolution of a partnership where the worker is employed by a partnership.

Redundancy

The principal reason for dismissal must be redundancy. Once the worker has established that he has been dismissed, his claim for a redundancy payment must succeed unless it can be shown (in practice by his employer) that he was dismissed for another reason. Redundancy occurs when the employer closes down his enterprise altogether, or closes down in the place where the worker is employed, or without closing down all or part of the enterprise there is a reduction in demand for work of a particular kind. The dismissed worker or workers may have taken part in industrial action against their employer, which has meant that the em-ployer's need for workers to do work of a particular kind is less. But that will not mean that he (or they) has not been dismissed for redundancy. 'Self-induced' redundancy is still redundancy.

Place of Employment

Two problems require a little further elucidation. The concept of 'place of employment' is often crucial. If a worker is employed as a shop assistant in Smith & Co.'s shop in Oxbridge, the place of employment will be that shop. If Smith & Co. close down their Oxbridge shop and offer to transfer the worker to London, he may be redundant. On the other hand, a worker might find that in his contract of employment he is described as a shop assistant employed by Smith & Co. 'to work in any of their shops'. In this case the place of work is any one of the shops owned by Smith & Co. in the United Kingdom, and closing one shop in Oxbridge is not an example of the closing down of the place where a particular person works. So there is no redundancy. This makes the description of the job in the contract of employment very important. The employer may want to describe it in very wide and general terms in order to avoid liability for redundancy payment. The worker may wish to describe the place of work in very narrow terms. Of course the express terms of the contract may be vague (as indeed may be the written statement issued to the worker under the Contract of Employment Act, 1972, see p. 36), and the scope of the concept of 'place of work' may have to be gathered from custom and practice.

Work of a Particular Kind

The other concept which is difficult is 'work of a particular kind'. Not every reduction of the work force for economic reasons causes redundancies. For instance, an employer who withdrew a free bus service which had been run to bring workers in from a considerable distance because fewer workers had to come from so far away, was held not to have caused redundancies. A great deal may depend upon how the claimant describes his job. In one case the claimant was an elderly (fifty-seven years old) barmaid who had been dismissed and replaced by a younger bunny-girl type in order to attract a different clientele. It was decided that there was no redundancy. The decision might have been different if the claimant, if not perhaps both parties, had described herself as a barmaid, and her replacement as a 'hostess' or 'bunny girl'. Of course, the question will often be one of degree, but there have been some surprising decisions, for example the skilled craftsman trained in using wood, who turned out to be too slow, careful and good a worker for modern times: no redundancy.

Alternative Jobs

The worker may lose his right to a redundancy payment if his employer either offers him his old job back on the same terms, or offers him a new and suitable job on different terms. If he unreasonably refuses either job, he loses his entitlement to all or part of a redundancy payment. A suitable job is defined as one which is not too markedly different from the previous one in the skills required, the pay, the responsibility, or the status. In deciding whether a refusal is unreasonable the personal circumstances of the worker may be considered. If he has already made arrangements to move to another town where jobs are more plentiful, it might be reasonable for him to refuse his former employer's offer. If the enterprise has changed ownership and the worker stays on working under the old terms or under new and suitable terms he is not entitled to a redundancy payment.

A redundancy payment may be payable in case of short-time and lay-off, but only if the worker has left the employment of his employer. In other words, the general rule is that no redundancy payment is due if employment continues.

Continuous Employment

A dismissed worker is not entitled to redundancy payment unless he has been continuously employed for at least two years since the age of eighteen. In order to qualify for entitlement to bring a claim for unfair dismissal he must have been continuously employed for twenty-six weeks. There are two basic threads in the notion of being continuously employed for a required period. One is that throughout a certain period there has been a contract of employment between the worker and his employer. The other is that the worker has been credited with units or periods of employment, each corresponding to a week during which the worker has actually worked, or been under a contract which normally involves the worker in working for sixteen hours per week. To be continuously employed for twenty-six weeks, a contract of employment must have been in existence for at least twenty-six weeks, and simultaneously the worker must have been credited with twenty-six periods or units of employment, each of one week involving work for sixteen hours.

There are certain qualifications of this general principle. First of all, if a week occurs during which the worker does not work or does not as usual work under his contract for sixteen hours (except where for not more than twenty-six weeks the worker is still normally bound to work at least eight hours a week), that week does not count and furthermore wipes out any weeks already credited to the worker. Similarly, if the contract of employment comes to an end that too wipes out any weeks already credited to the worker.

There are also exceptions. If in any week the worker spends any time engaged in strike action, that week (even though he may also work for sixteen hours) does not count as a period of employment, but it does not on the other hand wipe out weeks previously credited to him.

There are also cases where the contract has come to an end, but all the same, weeks already credited are not wiped out and can be used to bring a claim against the employer if the worker returns to work for him. The absence of a contract or the dismissal of the worker will not wipe out weeks already credited in the following conditions:

1. Any week during which the worker is unable to work because of sickness, pregnancy or injury (up to a maximum of twenty-six weeks).

2. Any week during which the employer's work temporarily ceases.

3. Any week during which the worker is still treated for some purposes as being employed (for instance, if he is still a member of the employer's pension fund).

4. Any week during which the worker is absent owing to pregnancy.

Periods of continuous employment by different employers may be added together in order to determine the worker's rights to compensation if dismissed by his latest employer. This applies when an employer acquires someone else's business as a going concern and keeps the workers on. The periods of employment are also added together when a worker is employed successively by companies which are jointly owned (or one of which owns the other).

Compensation

Once it has been established for what period the worker has been continuously employed by the employer by whom he has been dismissed for redundancy, the amount of compensation payable can be worked out. The maximum is about £2400. For each year of employment over the age of forty-one the worker is entitled to $1\frac{1}{2}$ weeks' pay. For each year of employment from twenty-two years up to and including forty years, he gets a week's pay, and for each year of employment between eighteen and twenty-one years, he gets half a week's pay. During his sixty-fifth year (the sixtieth year for women) the total amount due is reduced by one twelfth for each month as the sixty-fifth (sixtieth for women) birthday approaches, so that at sixty-five a man (sixty, a woman) is not entitled to redundancy compensation. A week's pay is calculated according to special rules, and only consists of pay for the amount of work the employee is obliged to do, and overtime the employee is obliged to work and the employer obliged to give.

The Worker's Three Claims

In every case of dismissal the worker may be able to bring one or more of the three principal claims we have discussed, that is, wrongful dismissal, unfair dismissal, or redundancy. In a sense the worker may enter three horses in the race, and he may win a prize with each. The fact that a worker is dismissed for redundancy and is awarded a redundancy payment will not necessarily prevent him from also being unfairly dismissed and therefore recovering compensation for that. An illustration is the case of *Vokes Ltd.* v. *Bear* (see pp. 65–6). A worker dismissed with notice for redundancy may get compensation for both wrongful dismissal and redundancy. But if he has already succeeded in a claim for unfair dismissal he may get no damages for wrongful dismissal because the unfair dismissal claim entitles him to compensation for loss of wages, which is what he would get for wrongful dismissal. He may have to content himself with the moral victory of having the court state that he was wrongfully dismissed. However, the court is likely to penalize him by making him pay the employer's costs of the case.

12. Safety at Work

Collective Bargaining

Safety at work ought to be regulated by collective bargaining. Indeed in certain industries and occupations there are highly developed and specialized forms of bargaining which regulate the safety of working conditions and practices, for example in the mastic asphalt industry, Post Office engineering and certain branches of the textile industry. However, until bargaining develops more widely, the basic standards of safety at work are in general established by law rather than by other means. If industrial action is taken over safety, it is not usually part of the pressure exerted by unions to bring about an acceptable bargain. Instead, it is a protest at the employer's failure to comply with safety legislation or in order to persuade the factory inspectorate to take action about unsafe working conditions.

Unions have from time to time taken a very active part in establishing statutory industrial safety standards. The best example is the Mines and Quarries Act, 1954, which is the best and most stringent piece of safety legislation we have. This is not simply because mining is a dangerous occupation, but because of the active determination of the National Union of Miners to secure adequate safety legislation.

However, the absence of safety legislation, for example, for shop and office workers (until 1963), is largely because of the weakness of trade union organization and the lack of trade union pressure for legislation.

Interest in safety varies very much from union to union, and the general level of official union interest in industrial safety is not great. The latest example of this is the enactment of the Health and Safety at Work Act, 1974, based on a Labour government's Bill, which was virtually an identical replica of a Bill introduced by the Conservative government in 1973.

In some ways this Act is a step backwards in the field of industrial safety. It is not progressive since it does not provide for a massive increase in the size of the inspectorate. This is essential for effective enforcement. It may reduce the number of situations in which an injured worker can sue for compensation from his employer when the latter is responsible for the accident. And in some instances it lightens the legal duty on the employer to secure the worker's safety. That legislation lessening the employer's obligations about safety in any way could be passed by a Labour government is an indication of the lack of serious interest taken by many trade unions in the subject.

Society seems to be quite content that many hundreds of workers should be killed at work annually and tens of thousands maimed. This is accepted with astonishing complacency even by the Labour movement. Clearly the legal rules and machinery for enforcement and the pressure exerted by trade unions are ineffective to deal with the problem. On the contrary, many industrial practices, such as various piece-rate systems, appear to contribute directly to the occurrence of accidents. Unhappily it is not always in the worker's own short-term economic interest that he should take as much care about his own safety as he ought.

The Basic Rules

The basic rules about safety at work fall under two heads: first of all, there are the judge-made rules, and secondly there are the rules laid down in statutes and statutory instruments. The judge-made rules were developed by the courts between 1880 and 1940, in a series of cases in which workers injured at work brought claims for damages for negligence against their employers.

Judge-Made Rules

The general principle established by the judges is that every employer is bound to take measures to protect his workers against unnecessary risk of injury, including contracting disease caused by conditions at work. The employer must take reasonable steps to choose workers who are not dangerous to their fellow workers. For instance, he should not employ someone who is not properly qualified to do the job he is employed to do, for example an incompetent crane driver. Nor should an employer knowingly take on someone whose character traits may expose others to danger, for example a dangerous practical joker; if a man develops such a trait, the employer must try to deter him from playing his dangerous pranks on his fellow workers.

The employer must also keep equipment in a reasonably safe condition. He must be careful to purchase tools and equipment from reputable suppliers, although he is not liable for latent defects which he cannot discover by examination. The manufacturer of defective equipment may be liable to pay damages for an injury caused by his negligence. The employer must plan the work; he provides premises which must be safe. He must plan how the work is to be done; in what order different processes are to occur, and where machines are to be placed. He must provide for the removal of waste matter and dust. He must supervise the work so that it is carried out reasonably safely.

The standard is that of the prudent employer. In practice, if an employer is doing less than is usual in the same industry, he is almost certainly doing less than he ought to as a reasonable employer. The fact that he is following the usual procedures and practices of the industry will often be sufficient to prove he is doing all that a reasonable employer would do. Sometimes, however, a judge may take the view that the danger of injury to workers is so great that what the average employer is doing to safeguard the worker is not sufficient, and is less than employers ought to be doing.

This common law duty of the employers is only practically important when a worker is injured. If the injured worker can show that the employer has broken the common law duty of care, and that the accident was caused by that breach of duty, the worker may be able to recover damages to compensate him for the economic loss caused by the accident. Mere proof of the employer's breach is insufficient. The court will want to be satisfied that if the employer had complied with the duty the accident would still have occurred. If the worker himself has shown less care for his own safety than the judge thinks he ought to have done, and that that lack of care has contributed to the accident, the judge can apportion blame between the worker and his employer. The judge can decide that the worker has suffered an injury which in money terms would entitle him to £100. He can then decide that the worker by his own carelessness was 50 per cent to blame, in which case the employer will be required to pay the worker only half the damages, that is, £50.

It is theoretically possible for a worker to obtain an order, known as an injunction, against his employer requiring him to comply with the common law standards of safety at work. If this order is issued and not complied with, it can be enforced by fine or imprisonment. Neither workers nor trade unions appear to have taken any interest in this possibility.

Statutory Rules

There are also rules embodied in statutes. In order to understand the statutory rules concerning safety, it is best to consider the position before the enactment of the Health and Safety at Work Act, 1974. Before this there were extensive rules established by the Factories Act, 1961, the Offices, Shops and Railway Premises Act, 1963, the Mines and Quarries Act, 1954, and a number of other Acts (and regulations made by ministers under these Acts) dealing with various occupations.

These rules did not, however, cover all occupations and there were several million workers who had no statutory protection whatsoever. Furthermore, for no very logical reason, the statutory rules laid down different standards for the safety of workers in different occupations, which were enforced by a number of safety inspectorates, often with little coordination. The penalties for non-compliance differed markedly from one statute to another. The position was complicated and confusing. The main defect of the whole system of rules about safety at work was that they were not successful, as the number of deaths and injuries at work was not being significantly reduced.

Enforcement of the Statutory Rules

The rules embodied in statutes were enforced by a number of different methods. The principal methods were as follows.

Criminal prosecutions

Breaking the statutory rules was a criminal offence. Prosecutions for breaking safety rules, under 2000 a year under the Factories Act, and the penalty, a fine of up to £300, was paltry. The average fine imposed was about £40, an amount which would have little deterrent effect. Clearly criminal prosecution did not ensure compliance with the law, because a small fine was irrelevant to employers indifferent to the legal requirements of safety law in the first place.

Inspection

There were at least half a dozen different inspectorates whose duty it was to see that employers complied with the law, and to prosecute them in case of default. Indeed, the number of inspectors has always been too small to cope with the task of regular inspection of all the premises within their jurisdiction. The collapse of the system of inspection for sheer lack of manpower gave rise to a philosophy which tried to make a virtue of the ineffectiveness of the inspectorate. The factory inspectors in particular tended to say that their most important function was educational; that all they could do was to guide and advise employers, and that they were more effective in this role if they did not act like policemen. The failure to enforce statutory safety standards gave rise not to an urgent demand for more inspectors, but to the growing view that all they could do was to advise, cajole, encourage and educate.

Claims for damages

Injured workers who could show that they had suffered an injury at work which they would not have suffered had the employer complied with a statutory safety rule could in many cases (but far from all) recover damages for what the lawyers called a breach of statutory duty. There were many of these claims, although the average amount of damages recovered was not high, some say of the order of £300.

Work-place representatives

There was no legal obligation that work-place representatives should be recognized as having some rights to enforce safety standards at work. The Mines and Quarries Act, 1954, was the sole exception. It gave miners the right to elect representatives who had the right to inspect mines; they were also allowed to see certain documents, thus ensuring compliance with safety rules; and they could examine the scene of any accident.

Safety supervisors

In certain industries employers used to be required to appoint safety supervisors whose job it was to see that employers complied with the law. Put like that it is easy to see what problems were raised. There was no special protection given to these safety supervisors against pressure from the employers. The law provided no protection against dismissal or discrimination if an employer thought that a safety supervisor performed his job over-zealously.

Safety committees

Apart from these methods there were safety committees with very varied functions which were established voluntarily in many industries and companies. There has been a steady increase in the number of these committees.

The Failure of Legal Rules

This system failed to make any serious inroads into the problem of industrial injuries for many reasons, some of which have been indicated.

The role of the courts should also be mentioned. In the early 1950s, for reasons difficult to understand, judges took the view that certain statutory reforms in the 1940s had unfairly tipped the balance in favour of injured workers because they had made it easier for injured workers to sue their employers successfully for damages for injuries caused by breach of the rules about safety at work. They therefore began to make it more difficult for workers to succeed in their claims. Some claimants' cases failed because it was not possible to prove that the cause of the accident was that the employer had not complied with his legal duty. Again the courts were only prepared to award damages if the injury suffered was the kind which the statutory rules had been established to guard against. In other words, the mere proof that the employer had broken the law, and that if he had not done so the accident would probably not have occurred, was insufficient. It might also be necessary to establish that the kind of accident was of the nature which the rule was intended to prevent.

The Health and Safety at Work Act

The Labour government intended the Health and Safety at Work Act, 1974, to deal with some of these problems. It makes some important improvements on the old system of the different ministries being responsible for safety at work, enforced by various inspectorates. There is a Safety Commission, which is entrusted with overall though not sole responsibility for safety. There is a single inspectorate under the control of the Commission, although two specialized inspectorates, the agricultural and the local authority, remain. Above all, statutory protection is extended to all workers in Great Britain (excluding Northern Ireland). The Act does not, however, apply to domestic employees in private households. The existing statutory rules continued to exist until replaced, and they must be replaced by further regulations or by approved codes. Approved safety codes may have any source, such as a collective agreement, or a statement issued by the British Standards Institute saying what in their opinion the interests of safety require. They are not law themselves, but can help to establish criminal or civil liability in legal proceedings. This is not unlike the role of the Code in unfair dismissals cases (see pp. 63–5).

The provisions of the Act

All employers are subject to certain general duties. These are defined in Section 2 of the Act as follows.

It is every employer's duty to ensure, as far as reasonably practicable, the health, safety and welfare at work of all his employees.

The matters to which that duty extends, without prejudice, include:

1. The provision and maintenance of plant and systems of work that are, as far as reasonably practicable, safe and without risks to health.

2. Arrangements for ensuring, also as far as reasonably practicable, safety and absence of risks to health in connection with the use, handling, storage and transport of articles and substances.

3. The provision of all necessary information, instruction, training and supervision to ensure, as far as is reasonably practicable, the health and safety at work of his employees.

4. The maintenance of any place of work under the employer's control in a condition that is safe and without health risks, as well as the provision and maintenance of entrances and exits that are safe and without health risks.

5. The provision and maintenance of a working environment for his employees that is safe, without risks to health, and with adequate facilities and arrangements for welfare.

Under the Act the Minister may provide for the trade unions to appoint safety representatives to be elected who will consult with employers and perform any other functions as the Minister may prescribe. These terms are very important.

Employers are legally obliged to establish safety committees if requested by the safety representatives.

The new safety inspectorate is given important additional powers, in particular that of serving a notice on an employer to improve his standards so as to bring them into line with the legal requirements. The inspectorate can also issue a prohibition notice. This means that the operations to which the notice relates, which carry a risk of serious personal injury, cannot lawfully be continued until the breach of the law is dealt with.

Weaknesses of the Act

Clearly these provisions are an improvement. However, there are certain important criticisms to be made.

First of all, there is no mention of substantially increasing the number of inspectors; the whole philosophy underlying the Act appears to involve continuing the policy of leaning against any large-scale prosecution of offenders.

Secondly, the Act has not dealt with the problem of bringing home to large corporations – which is what most occupiers of industrial premises are – the necessity for complying with the law. The Act increases the amount of the fine that can be imposed in proceedings before magistrates to £400. In proceedings before a jury the amount of the fine is unlimited and individuals can be sent to prison for up to two years. A company cannot be sent to prison, and it seems that a better method must be found of penalizing defaulting companies than the mere imposition of a fine, which past experience suggests will still be small, even though now there may be no formal upper limit. It is true that the Act permits proceedings to be taken against an individual director or manager of a company, if the breach of the law is due to his neglect. But unless the law makes directors personally obliged to comply with the regulations, this may not help much.

The third criticism is that workers injured as a result of an employer's failure to comply with the obligations listed in Section 2 (see p. 86) cannot claim damages for breach of statutory duty. Furthermore, the Act permits the Minister making regulations to insert a provision that no claims for damages can be brought by workers injured as a result of non-compliance with the terms of the regulations.

Lastly, the general duties laid down are to do certain things for the safety of the worker as far as they are *reasonably practicable*. This is a standard which falls below some of the existing standards, because in deciding what is reasonably practicable the employer may weigh up the cost of removing a danger against the risk of an accident occurring. Too much will depend upon the courts' view of what is reasonably practicable.

There is plenty of scope for improvement in the law about safety at work. Unfortunately, radical reform will have to wait until the trade union and Labour movement concerns itself more urgently with the problem than it has done in the recent past.

13. How Workers Can Get Their Rights

The basic answer to the question, 'How do workers get their rights?' is by organization, through union negotiation and action. The result is often crystallized not only in collective bargains, which in their turn may become part of the individual workers' own contracts, but also in legislation. Once rights have been embodied in legal forms, whether in contracts or legislation, they can be enforced by legal means if workers and their unions wish. What the worker himself can do, if he wants to avail himself of legal machinery to enforce his rights, runs as follows.

Claims over rights embodied in the contract of employment

The worker can sue the employer for damages for failing to comply with the express or implied provisions of the contract. If he has been dismissed he can sue for damages. If the amount claimed is under £1000 the claim can be brought in the County Court and will be heard by a County Court judge. If it is a 'small claim', that is, under £100, the County Court registrar can decide the case quite informally, and the procedure is quite easy. The registrar of the County Court can advise on the forms to be completed. If the amount claimed is more than £1000 it will usually be brought in the High Court, and it is difficult for a person to bring a claim himself there. Claims for personal injury must be brought within three years. Claims for breach of contract generally and for arrears of wages must be brought within six years.

Claims for unfair dismissal

These are brought in the industrial tribunal. The dismissed worker must send his claim to the Central Office of the Industrial Tribunals (see Appendix 2) so that it is received within three months of the dismissal. It is best in fact to make the claim on the form IT1 (a copy of which can be obtained form the local employment exchange). It is best to claim both for redundancy and for unfair dismissal.

Claims for redundancy payment

These are also brought in industrial tribunals. A claim for payment should be made and presented to the employer within six months of dismissal. If the employer refuses to pay or pays less than he ought, a claim should be made to the Central Office of the Industrial Tribunals within six months of dismissal.

Claims for social security benefits

Claims for unemployment benefit, sickness benefit and injury benefit are decided by local insurance offices. The worker claims for unemployment benefit by going to the local employment exchange, giving his National Insurance number and registering for employment. A claim must be made on the first day of unemployment, otherwise benefit may be lost. For sickness benefit the worker must get a medical certificate from his doctor, complete it and take or send it to the local Social Security Office. This should be done within six days of falling sick or being injured. For injury benefit the worker should inform his employer of the accident and make his claim at the local Social Security Office by sending a completed medical certificate which he can get from his doctor. This should be done within six days of the accident.

Leaflets explaining the rules governing qualification, disqualification and the procedure for how to get social security benefits can be obtained from local post offices, the local Social Security Office, the local employment exchange or the Department of Health and Social Security. Leaflets describing the rules governing entitlement to compensation for unfair dismissal and for redundancy payments can be obtained from the local employment exchange or from the Department of Employment.

Suggestions for Further Reading

The object of further reading is not to enable the reader to become an expert lawyer. If expert legal advice is to be sought, it should in the first place be sought from the union's legal service. The aim of the suggestions below is to help to deepen the reader's understanding of the role of law in labour relations and to help him to understand the basic legal rules which govern some of the more common problems arising out of the job situation. Those books marked with an asterisk have themselves got a useful bibliography.

A general, but conventional, account of the English legal system can be found in O. Hood Phillips, *A First Book of English Law* (Sweet & Maxwell, 1970), 6th ed.

A good guide for particular topics is B. A. Hepple, J. Neeson and P. O'Higgins, *A Bibliography of Literature Relating to British and Irish Labour Law* (Mansell, 1975).

There are two books which give an understanding of the role of law in labour relations. The first is K. W. Wedderburn, *The Worker and the Law** (Penguin, 1971), 2nd ed. It is out-of-date, but it does give a good insight into basic issues. O. Kahn-Freund, *Labour and the Law* (Sweet & Maxwell, 1972), is more difficult reading, but very valuable.

The basic statutes, summaries of the more important decisions of courts, as well as an up-to-date outline of the law covered in this book will be found in B. A. Hepple and P. O'Higgins, *Encyclopaedia of Labour Relations Law** (Sweet & Maxwell, 1972), two volumes, which is kept up-to-date by supplements six times a year. This is a work of reference.

A good account of labour law, specifically designed for trade unionists, is R. W. Rideout, *Trade Unions and the Law* (Allen & Unwin, 1973). Part IV of this book is specially relevant.

There are several useful general textbooks of labour law, although they are all somewhat out-of-date and there should be new editions soon: Charles D. Drake, *Labour Law* (Sweet &

Maxwell, 1973), 2nd ed.; O. Aikin and J. Reid, *Labour Law 1: Employment, Welfare and Safety* (Penguin, 1971); R. W. Rideout, *Principles of Labour Law* (Sweet & Maxwell, 1972), and Michael Wright, *Labour Law* (McDonald & Evans, 1974).

There are two stimulating works about safety at work that can be strongly recommended: John L. Williams, *Accidents and Ill Health at Work* (Staple Press, 1960), and Patrick Kinnersley, *The Hazards of Work: How to Fight Them* (Pluto Press, 1973).

On unfair dismissal the best accounts are S. D. Anderman, *Unfair Dismissals and the Law* (Institute of Personnel Management, 1973), and D. Jackson, *Unfair Dismissal* (Cambridge University Press, 1900).

On questions of social security the following can be recommended: H. Calvert, *Social Security Law* (Sweet & Maxwell, 1974). This is good for detail but is sometimes surprisingly uncritical. On supplementary benefit the best work is Tony Lynes, *Penguin Guide to Supplementary Benefits* (Penguin, 1973), 2nd ed.

Appendix 1. Legal Aid and Advice

The state Legal Aid and Advice system was first established under the Legal Aid and Advice Act, 1949. It has been much improved by the Legal Advice and Assistance Act, 1972. Three kinds of help are available, subject to certain conditions.

Legal advice and assistance

A member of the public who fulfils certain financial conditions is entitled to receive free (or partially free) advice and assistance from a solicitor up to the value of £25. This scheme is accordingly referred to as the £25 Scheme. A solicitor may write letters; he may negotiate on behalf of the person seeking his help; he may give legal advice; he can obtain legal opinions from barristers; he may draw up documents or take statements from witnesses. He cannot represent anyone in a court or tribunal. However, under the £25 Scheme he can help someone who intends to appear for a worker in any claim before an industrial tribunal. Details of the names and addresses of solicitors in any particular area providing their services under the £25 Scheme can be obtained either from the Law Society, 113 Chancery Lane, London WC2, or from a local Citizens' Advice Bureau.

Anyone seeking advice under the £25 Scheme has to fill in a Green Form obtainable from a solicitor giving advice under the Scheme. Details of income have to be given on the Green Form. Advice is free if the person's 'weekly disposable income' is less than £12·50. ('Disposable income' means the weekly wage after deducting income tax, National Insurance contributions and certain sums in respect of dependants and children.) Partly free advice is available to those whose 'disposable income' is not more than £24·50. Few workers in fact will qualify for wholly free advice if they are still at work, but quite a few may qualify for partly free advice. Partly free means that one will have to pay a contribution towards the cost of the solicitor's services.

Legal aid for civil court proceedings

This covers everything up to and including representation in a court by a solicitor or barrister. It is available for proceedings in all civil courts, but not industrial tribunals. A form (obtainable from a solicitor) has to be completed on which one has to give details of one's financial situation. The financial limits on free and partly free services are higher than under the £25 Scheme.

Legal aid in criminal court proceedings

The rules governing free representation by a solicitor or barrister in criminal proceedings differ from those in civil proceedings. Advice should be asked for from the clerk of the court concerned. There are no fixed financial limits to qualifying for free or partly free representation in criminal proceedings. The general principle is that one must show that one needs financial assistance in order to be adequately defended.

Appendix 2. Useful Addresses

Advisory, Conciliation and Arbitration Service. Head office: Cleland House, Page St, London SW1P 4NP. Tel: 01-222-4383. There are also eight regional offices.

Citizens Advice Bureau. Look in your local telephone directory under Citizens Advice Bureau.

County Court. For your local County see local telephone directory under 'Courts'.

Department of Employment. Headquarters: 8 St James's Square, London SW1Y 4JB. Tel: 01–214–6000.

Department of Health and Social Security. Headquarters: Alexander Fleming House, Elephant and Castle, London SE1. Tel: 01–407–5522. Copies of the Department's leaflets outlining rights to benefit and how to claim benefit can be obtained either from local post offices or from the Department of Health and Social Security, Leaflets Unit, Block 2, Government Buildings, Honeypot Lane, Stanmore, Middlesex HA7 1AY.

Employment Exchange. Look in your local telephone directory under 'Employment, Department of'.

Health and Safety Commission. Baynards House, 1 Chepstow Place, London W2 4TF. Tel: 01–229–3456.

Industrial Tribunals. Central Office: Central Office of the Industrial Tribunals (England and Wales), 93 Ebury Bridge Road, London SW1W 8RE. Tel: 01–730–9161. For Scotland: Central Office of the Industrial Tribunals (Scotland), St Andrew House, 141 West Nile St, Glasgow G1 3RU. Tel: 041–331–1601. There are also fourteen regional offices.

Social Security Office. Look in your local telephone directory under 'Health and Social Security, Department of'.

Supplementary Benefits. Enquire at your local Social Security Office.

Appendix 3. List of Court Decisions Referred to

Bent's Brewery Co. Ltd. v. *Hogan* [1945], Vol. 2 All England Law Reports, p. 570 (referred to on p. 48).

Gascol Conversions Ltd. v. *Mercer* [1974], Industrial Court Reports, p. 420 (referred to on p. 37).

Grieve v. *Imperial Tobacco Ltd., The Times* (newspaper) 30 April 1963 (referred to on pp. 31, 35).

Marshall v. *Harland & Wolff Ltd.* [1972], Industrial Court Reports, p. 97 (referred to on p. 50).

Rookes v. *Barnard* [1964], Appeal Cases Reports, p. 1129 (referred to on pp. 17, 21).

Sagar v. *Ridehalgh & Son Ltd.* [1931], Vol. 1 Chancery Reports, p. 310 (referred to on p. 55).

Vokes Ltd. v. *Bear* [1974], Industrial Court Reports, p. 1 (referred on on p. 65–6, 78).

Those cases marked with an asterisk can be found also in K. W. Wedderburn, *Cases and Materials on Labour Law* (Cambridge University Press, 1967).

Appendix 4. Complaint to an Industrial Tribunal

Industrial tribunals deal with some of the more important claims that a worker may bring against his employer, but not all. Claims for damages for injury at work and claims for wrongful dismissal have to be brought in the County Court or the High Court. In the near future claims for wrongful dismissal may be brought in an industrial tribunal, but at the moment they cannot.

Industrial tribunals deal with a wide range of claims, for instance for redundancy compensation (under the Redundancy Payments Act, 1965), for unfair dismissal (under the Trade Union and Labour Relations Act, 1974), for a correction in the written statement of the terms of employment issued by employers (under the Contracts of Employment Act, 1972), complaints of discrimination over recruitment and promotion on grounds of sex (under the Sex Discrimination Act, 1975), complaints of discrimination over pay and other conditions of employment on grounds of sex (under the Equal Pay Act, 1970), claims for maternity pay (under the Employment Protection Act, 1975).

A complaint *must* be made to the Secretary of the Tribunals, Central Office of Tribunals, in London, *by post at the earliest possible moment* if the matter to which the complaint refers occurred in England or Wales. If the complaint deals with something that happened in Scotland, it must be sent to the Scottish Central Office of the Industrial Tribunals in Glasgow. The complaint does not have to be couched in any particular form. All that is necessary is to state your name and address, your employer's name and address and what it is that you want the tribunal to get from the employer for you and why you think you are entitled to it.

However, there is an official form available from local offices of the Department of Employment, known as the IT1, which may make it easier for the claimant.

It is important not to strike out any of the Acts listed at the head of the form. You should leave it to the tribunal to decide what Act covers your case.

Illustration Acknowledgements

Camera Press page 15; Sport & General page 26;
Colin Smithson pages 28, 35; Camera Press page 43;
John Sturrock, Report page 52; Colin Smithson pages 57, 62;
Camera Press page 75; Topix page 79, Camera Press,
photo Alan Hutchinson page 88